SLOVAK
CONTEMPORARY
GLASS

Contents

Dan Klein – Foreword   5

Miroslav Zeman – Foreword   7

Katarína Beňová – Foreword   9

Sabina Jankovičová – The Slovak Contemporary Glass
and the Academy of Fine Arts and Design in Bratislava   10 – 29

The list of authors

Lubomír Artz   32 – 35

Miloš Balgavý   36 – 39

Marek Brincko   40 – 43

Václav Cigler   44 – 47

Eva Fišerová   48 – 51

Juraj Gavula   52 – 55

Ašot Haas   56 – 59

Pavol Hlôška   60 – 63

Patrik Illo   64 – 67

Andrej Jakab   68 – 71

Oliver Leššo   72 – 75

Pavol Macho   76 – 79

Lukáš Mjartan   80 – 83

Tomáš Ondroušek   84 – 87

Milan Opalka   88 – 91

Juraj Opršal   92 – 95

Viktor Oravec   96 – 99

Štepán Pala   100 – 103

Zora Palová   104 – 107

Lenka Šimonyiová   108 – 111

Jozef Tomečko   112 – 115

Vladimír Zbyňovský   116 – 119

Jan Zoričák   120 – 123

Askold Žačko   124 – 127

Select Bibliography   128 – 129

The List of Students at the Academy of Fine Arst and Design in Bratislava   130

Lubomír Artz, Glass composition, 2005

In her excellent survey of Slovak glass Sabina Jankovičová traces its development from the 1960s when Václav Cigler's dominant personality as a glass artist set the tone until the present day when young Slovak artists are influenced by different more current artistic trends. It is a hallmark of Slovakian glass art that it has always been closely linked to contemporary art capturing the mood of the moment in an art form that is sometimes too isolated. At the time when Václav Cigler was teaching in Bratislava Slovakian fine art was going through a very marked constructivisit phase and the glass creation that emerged from his class reflected that feeling for geometry and spatial arrangement. It used optical glass and optical cutting techniques to explore the inner and outer geometry of transparency, a material quality that is unique to glass. Cigler had a broad-minded approach to his subject and was as much a philosopher as a craftsman. He was a minimalist with a big heart and an open mind and his pupils were greatly influenced by his inspirational teaching. It is interesting that many of them ended up as artists working in materials other than glass.

As Jankovičová points out there are two different main streams in Slovak glass, the lyric and the geometric, although the geometric is perhaps the stronger of the two. The streams also flow in other directions making for great variety of styles within a small nation. But somehow Slovak glass retains a strong national identity which is both remarkable and very refreshing in this age of globalisation where everything tends to look alike. Even though there are as yet limited outlets for Slovak glass artists it is amazing how many of them there are and that they can all make a livelihood from their work. An impressive number of them are known internationally and have won important glass prizes. Among them is Zora Palová whose international career has involved teaching in Great Britain and winning a major prize at Coburg in 2006. Her work as well as that of Štepán Pala is in the Victoria & Albert Museum as well as in other major museum collections. Young artists like Oliver Leššo are also finding an audience far beyond national borders. Jan Zoričák and Vladimír Zbyňovský live in France and exhibit internationally, but their Slovak origins are very much recognised because of the nature of their work.

Whilst Václav Cigler's influence still remains the strongest the Bratislava School of Art has benefited from other fine teachers including Askold Žačko and Juraj Gavula, both distinguished artists in their own right. Each of them has brought something important to the Slovak glass scene, allowing it to broaden out whilst retaining a strong national identity. Štepán Pala and Pavel Hlôška, each in his own very different way, explore ideas connected with geometry, Pala in various different materials including wood and drawing. Juraj Opršal and Miloš Balgavý have both developed their own very distinctive language of optical geometry. Zora Palová, whilst retaining a geometric feeling in her work has moved towards a more lyrical, colourful and gestural kind of expression. Lukáš Mjartan also works in a vein which combines lyricism and geometry. An artist like Palo Macho is able to work in a very different, very personal idiom, whilst Patrik Illo has made his name in the world of design. All this adds up to a diverse yet very distinctive Slovak glass scene which is fast attracting worldwide recognition.

© **DAN KLEIN**
London May 2008

Václav Cigler, Cone, 2005

The present book, **Slovak Contemporary Glass**, aims at revealing the secrets of a material, which mankind has known and used for thousands of years. It is a book about glass and glass objects that spark so much curiosity and admiration all over the globe. Glass objects attract people by their beauty. The beauty radiates not only from the external form; it is enhanced by the magical energy of glass matter. And above all, there is ever present light – that tireless playmate of glass. The result of their mutual interaction are constantly changing images and effects that fascinate us people, and which remind us of the unknown secrets of nature and the outer world.

At the same time, this book portrays today's glass artists from Slovakia who can seize the secrets of this material and blow life in to it with their hands. Working with glass has a long tradition in Slovakia. It may be because this, at the same time, malleable and fragile material, inwardly rich and proud, is close the Slovak heart. This can be the reason why glass is docile in the hands of artists from Slovakia. This book also gives evidence that there are no worries about the continuation of the glass tradition in Slovakia. On the contrary, the new generation of glass artists further develops this already rich tradition by employing the latest technological procedures and adding their own creative qualities. Exceptional works of glass art from Slovakia are highly regarded worldwide and with no doubt they constitute a precious contribution to the world's cultural heritage.

Miro Zeman
Gallery NOVA

Pavol Hlôška, Pyramid, 1998

The book, **Slovak Contemporary Glass**, provides you with information on the development of glass art in Slovakia and on artists who use glass as their main creative material. The main text of Sabina Jankovičová describes the history and tradition of education at the Department of Glass at the Academy of Fine Arts and Design in Bratislava. This institution has shaped up and determined the position and development of glass in Slovakia since the 1960s. Sabina Jankovičová presents brief profiles of glass artists and their work; from the founder of the Department of Glass in Architecture, Václav Cigler, up to today's graduates of the Academy. She focuses also on artists from Slovakia who work abroad.

In addition, this book contains extended profiles of twenty four selected Slovak glass artists. This selection includes the heads of the Department of Glass at the Academy of Fine Arts and Design in Bratislava, Václav Cigler, Askold Žačko, Juraj Gavula and Viktor Oravec. It continues with presenting those personalities who have earned recognition far beyond the borders of Slovakia. Štepán Pala, Zora Palová, Pavol Hlôška, Miloš Balgavý, Lubomír Arzt are examples of artists with high international reputation. Also promising representatives of young generation of Slovak glass artists are included in the selection.

Katarína Beňová
E d i t o r

Contemporary Slovak Glass and the Academy of Fine Arts and Design in Bratislava

Sabina Jankovičová

Introduction

Contemporary Slovak glass is gaining growing awareness among the public and has become an item sought-after by private galleries and collectors, especially from abroad. Besides their own individual features, the work of Slovak glass artists present some common attributes that clearly point to the country of origin and the school to which they belong. Slovak glass is particularly valued for its specific approach towards glass material. This approach is a result of the artistic development having followed its own path.

Just as elsewhere, free glass creation in Slovakia can be traced back to the late 1960s. However, in Slovakia the development of studio glass has a background different from the rest of the world. Its quest for alternative methods of working with glass was determined by the centrally controlled society which did not support research in glass design and prevented artists from expressing their ideas. Artists sought for alternative possibilities for creation and handling of glass matter. Another important stimulus for the development of this discipline was the establishment of university education permitting realization of free glass artefacts.

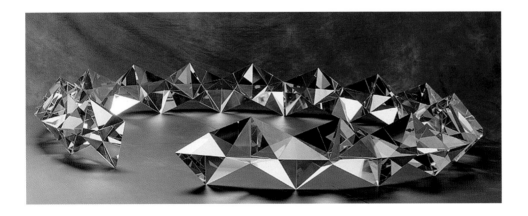

Štepán Pala, Crown of thorns, 1992

The Department of Glass in Architecture was founded at Bratislava's Academy of Fine Arts and Design in 1965. The arrival of the first students to this new department marked the beginning of free artistic glass-making in the country. Glass production hitherto associated with large glass companies and the design of functional glass now made its way into the privacy of the artists' studios.

Glass art in Slovakia displays distinctive features originating from diverse sources. The primary influence was the establishment and the clear and strong profile of the Department of Glass in Architecture. The course of Slovak glass art for years to come was predetermined by the concerted effort to shape a glass studio different from the Czech studios with its own specific identity and aided by the very strong personality of Václav Cigler, Head of the new department.

Hitherto, glass creation was represented by works of a few outstanding personalities, namely Karol Hološko and Jaroslav Taraba's design and Ľubomír Blecha's free work. Blecha's work constitutes an exceptional example of monumental sculpture using metallurgical techniques. Unfortunately, due to his relative isolation his work was not followed up.

The distinctive work of Slovak glass artists, especially in the 1970s and 1980s, is strikingly different from that of other countries. The specific character resides in the primary use of optical glass, geometric shapes, firm and undisturbed line, purity of glass matter, opening of inner virtual spaces by optical effects, and the use of the immanent properties of glass, such as transparency, reflectivity and also the ability to absorb light. These are the overriding characteristics of the work of the majority of artists. The 1980s witnessed a process of gradual enrichment by the introduction of new materials and techniques such as melted and sheet glass, structured surfaces, coloring and material combinations. The generation of the 1990s developed a conscious movement away from such a strict geometric canon. However, the tendency towards sobriety and making full use of glass properties has remained significant in the work of several representatives of the younger generation. The means of expression has become substantially wider for this generation.

Václav Cigler and the Department of Glass in Architecture

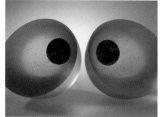

The Cigler School of Glass has become the accepted term when referring to glass art in Slovakia, not only to distinguish it from the Czech school but, mainly, when referring to the work of Cigler's students. Another description, the Bratislava Glass School, permits a broader understanding of glass art since it embraces the totality of its manifestations in the country.

The establishment of the Department of Glass in Architecture at Bratislava's Academy of Fine Arts and Design was conditional upon the pledge not to compete with its Prague counterpart headed up by Stanislav Libenský. The orientation of the new department towards the use of glass in architecture was intended simultaneously to address the need to construct monumental works in architecture. Through a selection process the Czech artist Václav Cigler was appointed Head of the Bratislava department.

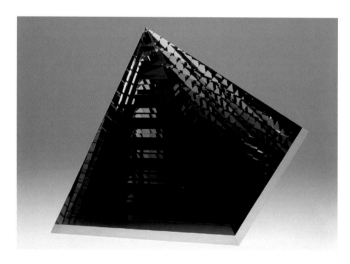

Václav Cigler (1929) was an individual who had freed himself from the Czech tradition of melted, sculpturally shaped glass which combined the expressivity of shape and colour. On the contrary, he moved towards neo-constructivism and minimalism and was developing conceptual and land-art projects. From the outset, his projects and works constituted a complex view on space, an attempt to create a new man-made architectural space in harmony with the surrounding environment. His works integrate and enrich the already existing world, constituting a reflection on the universe. Cigler strove to create a new composition, environment, space, and the balance and perfect harmony of the whole. These principles became fundamental and were conveyed to his students as part of their

　　　　Václav Cigler, Pyramid, 1997

education. Through his new position in Bratislava Cigler could pass on his ideas to create a new school based on his individual perception of thinking in glass, different from the glass art that dominated the Czech scene.

Václav Cigler was active in Bratislava until 1979. He built up the glass studio in Bratislava practically from scratch. His only tools were his own personal efforts, abundant enthusiasm and personal contacts with glassworks in all parts of Czechoslovakia, where he secured practical training for his students. Cigler's ultimate aim was to create a professional workplace at the Technical Glassworks in Bratislava. Here his students could design, study and work in direct contact with industrial production and with all the benefits of technological facilities. This plan, however, never came to fruition as Cigler failed to obtain the necessary support from national political institutions for this kind of noble ambition. Teaching at Cigler's department was very progressive for current socialist standards in Czechoslovakia. He encouraged his students to develop their own conceptual thinking and ability to stand up for their own designs. In this way, collective discussions among students and defending the objectives of the presented projects became an essential part of the teaching process. In addition to designs for architecture, which included lamps, dividing walls, stained glass, interior components, the students had to solve other design related tasks as well, like drinking glass, jewellery and free-style objects for interior and exterior. Studies of space using various materials played an equally important role. In these studies the students tested the possibilities of diverse materials, space relations, optimal working of shapes and overall compositions. They also had the opportunity to become familiar with various glass techniques such as blown, melted, technical, sheet and optical glass, and other materials such as plaster, stone, metal, Plexiglas.

At that time, design, jewellery and works for architecture were classified as applied art and, therefore, escaped ideological and political monitoring by the regime. Here, use of abstract means of expression was permissible that in other artistic disciplines was suspect. Cigler's personal approach was of particular importance for the future development of the students. Providing the students fulfilled the required tasks, he did not prevent them from exploring different domains of creative arts. They were given free rein to develop their ideas in the fields of geometry, constructivism, minimalism and conceptual art. Later this influenced their orientation significantly.

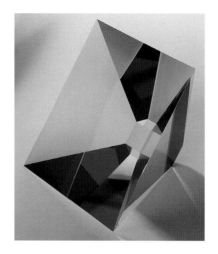

Department of Glass Design

In 1979, political pressures and, especially, personal differences with the university management forced Václav Cigler to resign as head of the department and return to Bohemia. Askold Žačko became Head of the department until 1989, maintaining its basic orientation towards design, architectural components and free creation in glass. Insufficient demand from the construction industry, due mainly to lack of financial resources, decreased the emphasis on research on compositions and space for architecture. This led to the department being renamed as Department of Glass Design. In the field of design, Žačko guided his students towards applied glass and jewellery. Thanks to his personal contacts, students could manufacture drinking glass sets at Slovak glassworks. For his own part, Žačko gradually liberated himself from that initial austere minimalism and geometry towards more expressive manifestations. The work of his students reflected this trend revealing a wider variety of forms, material combinations, colours and expression. However, some graduates still followed Cigler's work with optical glass.

In 1990, Juraj Gavula became Head of the Department of Glass Design. A sculptor himself, he used a variety of materials including glass. The legacy of Gavula is a more courageous combination of different materials including glass, metal, wood, plastic, and discarded objects. Installations employing mechanical motions of machines, liquids and light sources also display a forceful presence. Glass is placed in contrast with dissimilar elements suppressing the purely decorative function of aesthetic glass matter. Optical glass and its impressive properties lose their pre-

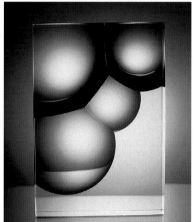

vious dominance that had led to stereotypes in shape and semantic emptiness. This new plurality of shapes and approaches gave impulse to a fresh heterogeneity in glass design. Many graduates finally abandoned glass completely in favour of other media.

In 2007 Viktor Oravec was appointed Head of the Department of Glass Design. He is a strong personality in performance and action art in Slovakia. He uses glass objects namely to create installations and/or as a part of performances.

In today's Slovakia, the graduates of these three concepts of teaching are active in a parallel plurality of expression. Organic and figurative shapes, disturbed surfaces and contours of glass objects have gradually superseded the geometry, minimalism and play with optical effects, which dominated the Slovak glass in 1970s and 1980s. Nevertheless, a tendency towards geometrical forms and the use of optical properties of glass are still present and dominate in the work of established artists.

In the 1970s, the artistic manifestation of Slovak glass artists evolved into two main streams, the lyric and the geometric. It is not always possible to determine a clear division between them. Some of the artists integrate colour to endow their work with a strong lyric tone. Today the term lyric may be replaced by the term structural, expressionist or gesture-like. However, the distinction between the two main streams remains a classification tool, since an overlap between the two streams may be observed.

The Geometric Stream

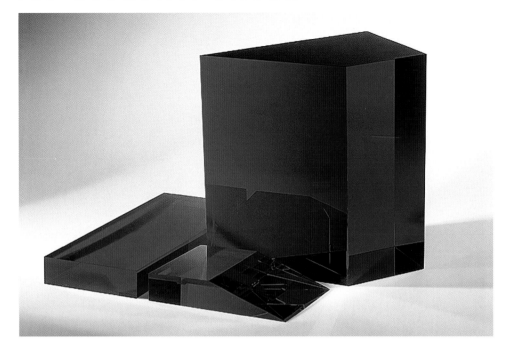

From the outset, the geometric stream was dominant in Bratislava's School of Glass because of the decisive influence of Cigler's department. Cigler's artistic vision was oriented towards minimalism and non-constructivism. He preferred basic, straightforward geometric shapes and subdued colour. An essential part of his work was the relation between a work of art and its environment.

On the other hand, his students originally focused on the inner space. The properties of optical glass permitted variations to resolve the problem of perfection of the virtual space within the object. For this reason, the Slovak glass embarked on a search for perfect shapes and purity of line. To capture space was the ultimate quest. Compositions of multiple bodies later replaced the individual objects the relation between the bodies resulted in a new field of research.

From the beginning, Jozef and Pavel Tomečko, Milan Gašpar, Eva Potfajová, Marián Mudroch, Askold Žačko, Juraj Gavula, Štepán Pala and others have worked principally with transparent optical glass of subdued colour. By means of cutting, grinding and polishing of the outer surfaces they created virtual space within. The artists took advantage of transparency, reflecting surfaces, and the movement of virtual spaces depending on the position of the viewer. The dominant element here

Miloš Balgavý, Red composition, 2005

is colourless glass or glass with colour of champagne: colour is suppressed to stress form. Form results from the search for perfection in the use of straight or curved lines. Besides basic forms, such as spheres, cubes, and prisms, the artists created new irregular bodies; tetrahedral and polyhedral structures of both square and round contours. Bowl-shaped segments imprinted into the glass have become a frequent theme.

In the work of some artists, the object consists of multiple elements or bodies distributed in space or on a flat glass substrate creating a spatial architecture. In composed objects of some artists the composition is essential, while for other artists the variability or mobility is paramount.

Gradually, the introduction of intense colour, opacity and mirrors disturbed the sobriety or sterility of the colourless bodies. In this way, the perfect solid outline of the shapes was destroyed. These tendencies became stronger during the course of the 1980s. In the 1990s some artists integrated structural tendencies by combining melted and optical glass or modified their original orientation towards a more heterogeneous expression. The artists who continued in geometric stream used sober shapes and optical effects to catch the attention of the viewer.

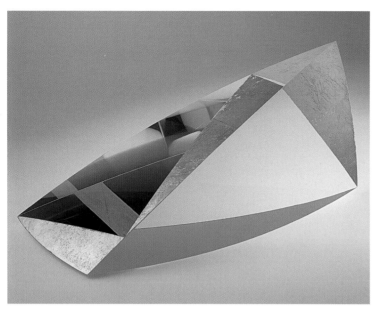

Miloš Balgavý (1955) continues in tradition of the Cigler School and remains faithful to sober forms, neat and compact shapes, and simple profiles. He enriches the geometric language by allowing colour to play an important role in his work. A frequent theme during the 1980s was the arrangement of identical objects of different or similar colour side by side. He investigated their mutual relationship, the effect of colour, transparency and opacity of glass on the whole effect of the composition. He further studied the variation of colour intensity in relation to the thickness of the object in using pyramid-like forms. In the 1990s, he focused his attention on the basic geometric shape of the sphere, which became the tool for expressing symbolic messages. The artist continued to make use of intense colour and optical properties of glass such as transparency, absorption and opacity. The sphere became an object by itself, intangible, either divided by a mirror surface or composed of two hemispheres of different colours. He created compositions using segments of the sphere and lenses, both shapes are combined in innumerable colour variations. Occasionally the artist employed polygonal geometric forms for compositions of colour glass.

Pavol Hlôška (1953) belongs to the followers of the sober geometry of the Cigler School and continues to investigate the inner space of the glass object. He employs the properties of optical glass and the effect of vacuum metallisation of individual glass pieces which form the final object. The pieces are glued together, and the outer surfaces of the object are then polished or given a matt finish. His favoured shapes are sober geometrical forms, such as a prism and lenses. The inner space is fractured into countless variations by the employment of metal surfaces. Reflections at these metal surfaces depend on the movement of the viewer resulting in the virtual motion of the inner space.

Oliver Leššo, White eye, 1998

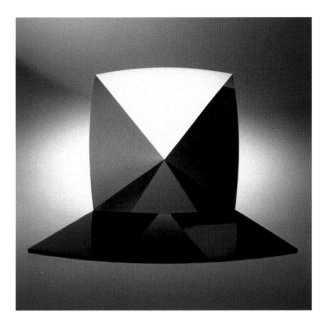

Juraj Opršal, La Lunette d'Approche, 2001

Geometrical purity, absolute use of transparency and optical effects characterize art works of **Lubomír Arzt** (1946). Arzt focuses on objects with sharp edges, firm and straight outlines, occasionally disrupted by a curvature. His favourite compositional element is a concave niche having a form of a hemisphere or a segment of sphere. He almost exclusively uses transparent, colourless, white or champagne optical glass. His compositions of multiple bodies rarely contain both colour and mirror-like surfaces.

Absolute, even sterile geometrical sobriety appears in the works of **Andrej Jakab** (1950). His objects are simple geometrical structures; that get the boost from a concave segment of sphere or a colour veil formed inside the glass matter.

The youngest representative of the geometric stream in Cigler's spirit is **Oliver Leššo** (1973). Leššo draws inspiration from examples of the older established artists; from their use of simple basic shapes. These are hemispheres, prisms, and discs. The inner structure and space of objects is important to him and therefore he rarely disrupts their surfaces and outline. The inner structure is shaped during the very process of the creation of the object, when small regular glass pieces are melted together. The boundaries between the pieces form a structure of a grid or a net that becomes visible in the bulk. Dynamic changes of the inner structure occur due to the optical effects appearing at the movement of the viewer. Leššo also works with colour but only in a limited range.

The following artists deviate from the sober geometry of the Cigler School. The work of **Milan Opalka** (1961) concentrates on varying the basic shape of a disc and a lens, which he arbitrarily combines into compositions of two objects. In these compositions Opalka investigates the relationship between transparent and opaque glass objects and the dynamics of their possible arrangements. He disturbs the purity of glass matter by incorporating colour details; the overall effects is harmonious.

Juraj Opršal (1953) strives in his work for new absolute geometric shapes of predominantly asymmetric outline and labile balance. Resulting objects are created by dynamic compositions of several bodies, or by a single object placed on a dark glass substrate with mirror-like effect. By different arrangement of the bodies, the artist shapes the space and creates tension in it. He combines contrasting colours and surfaces that underline the tension of the composition.

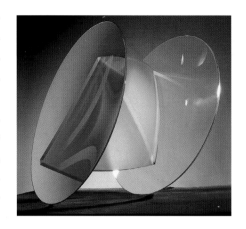

Štepán Pala (1944) based his work on the consistent application of mathematics. Geometry is not the eventual target for him; it is simply a means of revealing the hidden spaces of the universe. Pala develops and tests his ideas in drawings and three-dimensional objects made of wooden skewers. Glass is for him an additional material for expression. Glass objects can unveil the complexity of geometrical shapes; they follow the aesthetics of mathematics. Pala exhausts all possibilities of symmetrical and asymmetrical composition, dynamics and stability. He studies an influence of a small change in the composition on its overall effect. In the past Pala focused on the creation of variable compositions using prisms, rectangular blocks and other sober forms. He was interested in dynamics of compositions using lenses. He used heat to bend lenses and by creating asymmetric composition he enabled the body to move. At present, the artist combines colourless lenses with forms of colour melted glass. He inserts a composition of geometric or irregular forms between two monumental lenses producing a variety of optical effects. Complex structures of crystal-shaped formations from colour glass and spatial "drawings" by laser within a block of glass are additional fields of Pala's exploration.

There are several artists whose work balance between the geometry and expressive approach and who concentrate on the internal structures in glass matter. They work with veils of bubbles and colour that become visible in the transparent matter and accented by polished surfaces. **Drahomír Prihel** (1956) and **Ľubomír Ferko** (1956) are amongst these artists. The outer shape of their objects remains sober, while the inner space is a busy play of veils of bubbles and colours, and internal structures within the glass.

The Structural Stream

Gradually structural elements have found their way in to the works of Slovak glass artists who step by step have adapted their geometric program. This process is related to the departure from using the dominant technology of cold-processing of optical glass in favour of melted glass and other possible means of expression. The internal structure of the glass matter, vibrant and intense colour, surface structures, and/or contrasting effects of smooth and rough surfaces have become frequently exploited. Modelling of forms using gesture has also appeared.

Ľubomír Blecha (1933) is the first representative of the structural and expressive stream in the Slovak glass. However, his work remained isolated in the context of Slovak glass art. In the early 1960s, he already created reliefs from colour melted glass. In the process of creation, he was modelling surfaces of the relief by applying interventions and imprints, achieving a powerful expressive effect. Another area of his work was blown sculptures of organic shapes that substantiated the fluidity of glass. Glass cords were used to structure the inner space and reflections from a bubble-like surface gave the impression of movement. In addition to the colourless glass, Blecha partially integrated colour; smoky colour glass and cut ruby. In the 1980s, he focused on studying the movement in glass sculptures; when bent, glass mobile bars were placed on opaque mirror-like glass substrates.

One of the artists who abandoned the geometric sobriety of the Cigler School for an expressive manifestation was **Askold Žačko** (1946-1997). In the 1970s he already left the absolute sobriety of straight lines in favour of organic shapes. At first he maintained clear transparency and reduced colour as a major feature of his sculptures, later on he started using intense colour. Gradually, his interventions into the surface of his sculptures became more aggressive, the glass matter was broken by open perforations. He brought into contrast smooth surfaces with rough structures, straight lines against irregular ones, resembling broken edges. The tension of the composition was underlined by the asymmetry of the object that rested on one point. Figurative themes replaced symbolic and lyrical ones. Žačko created extensive cycles, in which he focused on human heads and figurative themes. He abandoned the aestheticism of glass matter and the use of attractive optical effects of the glass object. He aimed at an expressive manifestation, devoid of any sentiment.

The work of **Juraj Steinhuebel** (1958) took a similar direction of Žačko. He employed a sculptural approach in creating glass artworks. Colour, structured surfaces, contrasting materials and figurative themes were the main features of his work.

Eva Fišerová (1947) inclined towards organic morphology already during her studies. In her diploma work, she made use of the internal structure of melted glass while keeping the surface smooth and intact. She gradually integrated colour and opaque glass, and started to disturb surfaces of the glass matter. Her glass objects are characterized by crystal-like structured surfaces and an asymmetrical expressive composition.

Eva Fišerová, Empty armour, 2007

Some of the specific characteristics of the Bratislava School of Glass are visible also in the work of **Jan Zoričák** (1944), although he studied in Prague and has lived in France since 1970. His early work reflected the geometry of the Cigler School; however, the Czech glass tradition has been present in his work from the beginning. The main features of his works comprise organic forms, intense colours, destruction of the shape, and the use of internal structures of glass, such as bubbles and veils.

Zora Palová (1947) gradually abandoned the geometry of optical glass in favour for expressive melted sculpture. The basic building element of her sculptures is an intense colour, which has become the determining means of expression. She fills the shapes, which are inspirations from the outside world of both nature and man, with colour creating symbols and totems of color and light. She combines smooth and rough surfaces in the final form, which are complemented by waves and curves, fingerprints, and tangible imprints. She uses polished surfaces that serve as openings for the observation of the internal structure of the colour glass matter.

The work of the young glass artist **Lukáš Mjartan** (1975) demonstrates a direct influence of the studio of Zora Palová. Mjartan also employs glass with an intense colour. His shapes are simple, compact, and with a self-contained outline. The glass matter is shaped into geometrical patterns. The objects of Mjartan balance between peace and tension that is achieved by combining thick and thin areas and by contrasting smooth and rough surfaces.

Different materials, found objects and light sources have been gradually implemented by many artists. Some have presented installations. A pioneer in this field was **Ján Mýtny** (1955). Mýtny created dynamic objects using colour and mirror-like effects by stacking glass sheets. In this way, he suppressed the static nature of objects and, at the same time, an empty aesthetics. The overall effect of the objects was somewhat technical. Later, he combined glass with other materials, minerals, discarded and found items. The compositions using these items as glass imprints of the real world had a strong expressive message and were devoted to environmental issues.

Combining different materials together was the main characteristic of the works of **Jozef Vachálek** (1944). He was one of the first graduates of Václav Cigler and was active not only as a glass artist but as a sculptor as well, creating works for architecture. Metal was a typical material he used for works in architecture. He combined metal and stone also in glass objects. In his work one can observe a shift from simple glass objects, where the inner space was a focus of attention, towards large objects fitting into the architectural space and installations.

Juraj Gavula (1942) has followed a journey of investigating different materials such as stone, wood, metal and glass in his art works. His early works were marked by Cigler's teaching and were characterized by purity of line and shape, and reduced colour. However, organic shapes of these objects were suggesting an escape from geometry. His glass objects used the expressive properties of melted glass, color, and rough surfaces. Above all, the combinations of glass with materials of completely different properties result in tension between fragile and solid, transparent and opaque, colour and colourless.

Mária Hajnová (1958) used melted colour glass for creating distinct symbolic objects. She also worked with colour blown and sheet glass, often combining it with contrasting materials such as wood and metal.

The use of materials different from glass and their integration into overall composition characterize the work of many representatives of young generation of artists. Martin Masarovič and František Csandal imprinted elements of nature such as stone or wood into the glass matter. The overall effect of their works is based on the contrast of different materials. **František Csandal** (1966) worked with intense colour of glass and surface imprints such as the growth rings of wood. **Martin Masarovič** (1968) often integrated round-shaped stones into the glass matter, which resembled a foreign intervention.

A similar principle of breathing life into glass matter characterizes the work of **Vladimír Zbyňovský** (1964). Zbyňovský lives in France where he has brought his experience from the Glass Design studio at the Academy of Fine Arts and Design in Bratislava. In many respects his work follows the tradition of the Cigler School, above all in his respect for spectacular properties of glass. He combines stone blocks of a distinct surface with glass matter. The peculiarity of his objects is based on the combination of a smooth, viscous, as if molten block of optical glass with a rigid, stationary, and non-transparent stone matter. Glass perfectly emulates the rough surface of the stone. Making use of the optical properties of glass he magnifies the roughness of the stone surface, creating an extraordinary landscape that underlines the contrast of the interface between the two materials.

 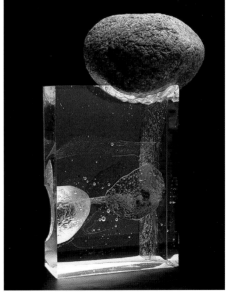

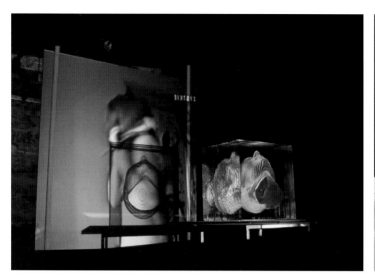

Paľo Macho (1965) is a distinctive artist who uses the technique of heat shaped sheet glass combined with painting on glass. The important elements in his works are a surface texture, colour, and a painting gesture. His works are objects and paintings at the same time and demostrate the artist's close relationship to contemporary abstract and geometrical visual art.

The youngest generation of glass artists moves away from the glass artefact as a solitary object. Plurality in the approach to glass as a material dominates their work. Glass has become just one of the possibilities of artistic expression. They present installations, combinations of materials, use of light sources, water, machine movements and multimedia elements. Artists who entered the art scene in the mid 1990s brought this new dimension into glass creation, which, since then, has lost its exclusive orientation towards cut optical glass. **Matej Gavula** (1972), **Peter Ondrušek** (1973) and **Patrik Kovačovský** (1970) were amongst to the most outstanding representatives of the mid 1990s. They introduced neo-conceptual and neo-constructivist approaches and eventually have become the representatives of Slovak contemporary art without any particular relation to glass material.

The work of **Patrik Illo** (1973) escapes the traditional orientation towards free glass creation in Slovakia. Above all, Illo is a designer. Glass is the material that permits him to create a perfect shape for an applied-art object. His designs follow the traditional form or can be of completely innovative shape, containing a new witty and playful detail enriching the traditional form. For many years, Patrik Illo has cooperated with the glass factory Rona in Lednické Rovne, for which he designed sets of drinking glasses and other tableware. More recently, Illo has been working with the

← **Martin Múranica**, Installation, 2007   **Tomáš Ondroušek**, Time bomb, 2007

Polish glassworks in Krosna applying new techniques, mainly melted glass. For his latest series of applied-art vessels he has used colour glass with a transparent surface layer, in which regular bubble patterns are visualized.

The youngest graduates of Gavula's glass studio continue to develop these trends. Although some of them have picked up the Cigler's example (Marek Brincko, Lenka Šimónyiová), the expressive, structural tendencies, the sculptural approach and installations dominate their creative work.

Early objects of **Marek Brincko** (1981) fit into the geometric stream of the Slovak glass. He focused on the transparency of the glass matter and the optical effect of precisely shaped objects. Since then, he has implemented expressive means of manifestation. Colour and sculptural approach have become important factors in his work and he has turned his attention to the outer world as the source of inspiration.

Lenka Šimonyiová (1981) has developed her own distinctive style of creative work. Although her creative approach follows the geometric stream, she surpasses and enriches it. The basic principle for building up her compositions is stacking the strips of optical glass on top of each other. The individual strips are placed perpendicularly against each other in such a way that an empty space is formed between the transparent strips. The shapes of the strictly geometric objects are only indicated since the full objects is a combination of glass pieces and empty spaces. This combination of matter and empty spaces creates a fascinating moment and tension in her works. Colour and the optical effects at the edges of glass sheets enrich the sensual experience for the viewer.

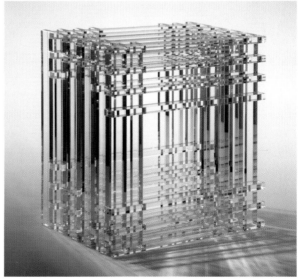

Ašot Haas (1981) also follows the geometric stream, namely by applying the constructivist and minimalist tendencies. He places with precision small metal particles in between sheets of glass to give form to a geometric-like object immersed in glass. The form of the object is not unambiguous; it is ephemeral and changes as the viewer moves. The compositions of Haas appear technical and sober, creating architectural space. His other works integrate mechanical machines that provide the objects with motion. These technical components are in strong contrast to a glass carrier.

Martin Múranica (1980) has adopted a sculptural approach towards glass and has avoided the decorative aesthetics of the material. Múranica has developed both figurative and abstract line in his work. He uses artificial light and film projection in the figurative compositions, mainly themes of human heads and faces. In situ installations, which are witty comments on the natural and industrial environment, constitute a significant part of his work. He integrates the natural elements in the installations such as light, darkness, water, earth, and vegetation. Maja Štefančíková (1978) creates works that are intended as absurd comments on everyday reality. Štefančíková uses contrasting combinations of glass and natural materials, found objects, photographs, and light sources. Ján Gašparovič (1981) looks for new sources of energy, mainly mechanical ones, which he incorporates into his objects. He uses materials that contrast glass such as colour liquids or parts of mechanical machines.

Tomáš Ondroušek (1985) integrates technical parts into glass cases, representing bombs, with a mysterious content. Mechanical mechanisms and light sources are placed inside the cases that illuminate and animate the glass matter. It is not the aesthetic effect of glass but, on the contrary, its expressive qualities that stand in the focus of Ondroušek's interest. The expressive qualities are underlined by

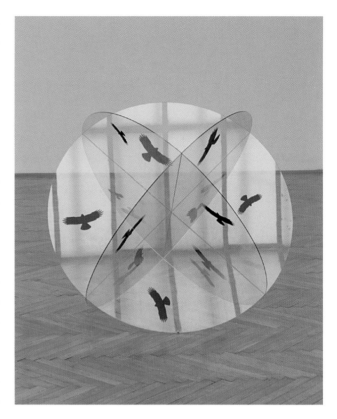

↑ **Matej Gavula**, Enter, 1994   **Ján Gašparovič**, 3D (Machine of Seeing), 2004   **Andrej Jančovič**, Small connection, 2007

the use of colour light and foreign materials. **Ivan Illovský** (1978) also represents the line of the denial of decorative aesthetics of glass matter. However, glass in his compositions maintains its purity. Illovský creates compositions of blocks of glass with used corroded metal parts. These found ready-mades stand in direct opposition to the glass block, which Illovský carefully processes. Sometimes they add an additional function; they are little wheels that allow the object to move. In his recent works Illovský cast the metal parts in glass to give them an ephemeral imprint of reality. Similarly, **Andrej Jančovič** (1986) employs ready-made objects and makes their imprints into the glass matter. The contrast between the sobriety of the blocks of glass and the shape of the imprinted objects bring tension into his compositions.

Conclusion

At present, the Slovak glass art is a heterogeneous area of the creative art. Slovak glass owes its specific character to its individual development originating from the tradition established by Václav Cigler. The tradition of the Cigler School dominates in the work of the established artists and is characterized by the employment of the geometry. However, this characteristic feature disperses in the spectrum of various other means of expression. In parallel to this geometric stream, the structural and expressive tendencies together with the post-modern sculptural expressions that combine materials, installations and new media are developed. The work of Slovak glass artists has become as heterogeneous and multilayered as anywhere else in the world.

Ladislav Pagáč, Fragment, 1999 (1. Slovak Invest Company)

Lubomír Artz

Miloš Balgavý

Marek Brincko

Václav Cigler

Eva Fišerová

Juraj Gavula

Ašot Haas

Pavol Hlôška

Patrik Illo

Andrej Jakab

Oliver Leššo

Palo Macho

Lukáš Mjartan

Tomáš Ondroušek

Milan Opalka

Juraj Opršal

Viktor Oravec

Štepán Pala

Zora Palová

Lenka Šimonyiová

Jozef Tomečko

Vladimír Zbyňovský

Ján Zoričák

Askold Žačko

Lubomír Artz

1946, Prašice, SK

Geometrical purity, absolute use of transparency and optical effects characterize art works of Lubomír Arzt. He focuses on objects of austere forms and shapes with sharp edges, firm and straight outlines, occasionally disrupted by a curvature. A concave niche having a form of a hemisphere or a segment of sphere is a favourite compositional element that is present in his objects. He almost exclusively uses transparent, colourless, white or champagne optical glass. It is the multiple reflection from polished surfaces and incorporation of colour that generate intriguing and colourful multi-dimensional inner spaces.

1960 – 64   Secondary School of Applied Arts of Glass, Železný Brod, CZ

Individual exhibitions (selection):
1994   Gallery Broft, Eidnhoven, NL
                Gallery Groll, Naarden, NL
1993   Essener Glass Gallery, Essen, D
1991   Galerie D'Amon, Paris, F
                The Glass Art Gallery, Toronto, CAN

Group exhibitions (selection):
2007   Contemporary Slovak Glass, Leo Kaplan Modern Gallery,
                New York, USA
2006   Gallery NOVA, Bratislava, SK
                St'Art, Gallery NOVA, Strasbourg, F
2005   Glaskunst, Galerie des Beaux Arts, Heeze, NL
                Thinking in Glass, Václav Cigler and His School, Gemeentemuseum, The Hague, NL
1990   Galerie Rob van den Doel, The Hague, NL
                Glassgalerie Klute, Vienna, A
1989   Galerie Rob van den Doel, The Hague, NL

Representation in public collections (selection):
Ministry of Culture of Slovak Republic, Bratislava, SK
Slovak National Gallery, Bratislava, SK
Glassmuseum, Ebeltoft, D
Museum of Glass and Jewelers, Jablonec nad Nisou, CZ
Museum Sars Poteries, Sars, F
Gallery NOVA, Bratislava, SK

OBJECT, 2002

OBJECT (YELLOW), 1998

ASTRUS, 1995 (Jonker – Zaremba collection, NL)

Miloš Balgavý

1955, Bratislava, SK

Miloš Balgavý continues in tradition of the Cigler School and remains faithful to sober forms, neat and compact shapes. His work is eminent by the perfection of execution and demands attention. Beauty radiates from refined yet simple geometric forms, such as pyramid, cube, sphere, and their segments. He enriches the geometric language by allowing colour to play an important role in his work. Balgavý makes use of intense colour and optical properties of glass such as transparency, absorption and opacity. He focuses his attention on the basic geometric shape of the sphere, which has become the tool for expressing symbolic messages.

1970 – 1974   Secondary School of Applied Arts, Bratislava, SK
1978 – 1984   Academy of Fine Arts and Design, Bratislava, SK
                Department of Glass Design (V. Cigler, A. Žačko)

Solo Exhibitions (selection):
2008   De Twee Pauwen, The Hague, NL
2006   Light of Colors III. – Retrospective, West-Slovak museum, Trnava, SK
2004   Gallery NOVA, Bratislava, SK
2003   Studio A/D/A, Trnava, SK
2002   Glass Gallery DIVYD, Hummel Museum, Bratislava, SK
                Gallery Plateaux (together with P. Hlôška), London, GB
2001   Gallery Groll, Naarden, NL
                Etiene & van den Doel Gallery (together with P. Bremers), Gulpen, NL
1999   Rob van den Doel Gallery, The Hague, NL
                Municipal Gallery, Mirbach Palace, Bratislava, SK
1997   Vermes Vila, Slovak National Gallery, Dunajská Streda, SK

Group Exhibitions (selection):
2007   Contemporary Slovak Glass, Leo Kaplan Modern Gallery, New York, USA
2006   Glaskunst, Galerie des Beaux Arts, Heeze, NL
2005   Thinking in Glass, Václav Cigler and His School, Gemeentemuseum, The Hague, NL
2004   Hommage aan Rob van den Doel, Etiene & Van den Doel Galerie, Oisterwijk, NL
                Collect, V&A Museum, London, GB
2002   Dialogo con la luce, Cristallo Slovaco Contemporaneo, Gallery Via Larga,
                Florence, Roma, I
2001   Reflecties, Gallery Groll, Nieuweigein, NL

Representation in public collections (selection):
Museum van den Togt, Amsterdam, NL
Museé des Arts Décoratifs, Lausanne, CH
Glassmuseum, Ebeltoft, D
Nationale Nederlanden, Rotterdam, NL
Slovak National Gallery, Bratislava, SK
Gallery NOVA, Bratislava, SK
Museum of Applied Arts, Prague, CZ

BIRD, 1993

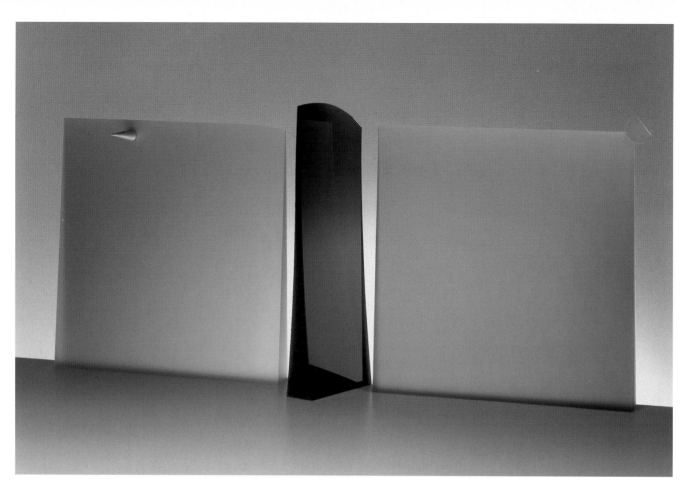

PICTURE I., 1995

FLOWER, 2006

SUNSET OF GODS, 1993 (Jonker – Zaremba collection, NL)

Marek Brincko

1981, Levoča, SK

Marek Brincko belongs to the youngest generation of Slovak glass artists. His early objects fit into the geometric stream of the Slovak glass and demonstrate the influence of years spent in the studio of Pala and Palova. Here he focused on the transparency of the glass matter and the optical effect of precisely shaped objects. Since then, he has implemented expressive means of manifestation. Colour and sculptural approach have become important factors in his work and he has turned his attention to the outer world as the source of inspiration. His works are not only pleasant for eyes but invite for contemplation.

1995 – 1999   Secondary Technical School of Wood, Spišská Nová Ves, SK
2000 – 2006   Academy of Fine Arts and Design, Bratislava, SK
                    Department of Glass Design (J. Gavula), trained by private studies by Š. Pala

Solo exhibition:
2008   Gallery NOVA, Bratislava, SK

Group exhibition:
2008   Gallery M. P. Visser, 's-Hertogenbosch, NL
                    Talente, Munich, D
                    Talente, Gallery X, Bratislava, SK
2007   St'Art, Gallery NOVA, Strassbourg, F
                    Finalist of the Gallery NOVA Award Glass 2007, Gallery Z, Bratislava, SK
2006   Galerie u Prstenu, Prague, CZ
2005   Gallery NOVA, Bratislava, SK
2004   Young Artists from High Tatras, Kežmarok, SK

ICEBERG, 2007

LITTLE DOG, 2007

UNICORN, 2008

Václav Cigler

1929, Vsetín, CZ

Václav Cigler is a world renowned artist who has contributed a new destination for glass application – the creation of works of art. He applied neo-constructivism and minimalism to his work and was developing conceptual and land-art projects. From the outset, his projects and works constituted a complex view on space, an attempt to create a new man-made architectural space in perfect harmony with the surrounding environment. These principles became fundamental and laid foundations to a new school based on his individual perception of thinking in glass. Cigler's objects inspire contemplation and search for spirituality, conscience and truth.

1948 – 1951	Secondary School of Applied Arts of Glass, Nový Bor, CZ
1951 – 1957	Academy of Fine Arts, Prague, CZ
1965 – 1979	Founder and Head of the Department of Glass in Architecture at the Academy of Fine Arts and Design in Bratislava, SK

Solo Exhibitions (selection):

2006	Gallery NOVA, Bratislava, SK
2004	Gallery of Benedikt Rejt, Louny, CZ
	National Gallery, Prague, CZ
2003	Gallery Pokorná, Prague, CZ
2000	Palace of Family Lichtenstein, Prague, CZ
1999	Gallery Friedman, New York, USA
	Gallery at Jánsky Hill, Prague, CZ
1997	Moravian Gallery, Brno, CZ
1993	Rob van den Doel Gallery, The Hague, NL
	Mánes, Prague, CZ
	National Gallery, Prague, CZ

Group Exhibitions (selection):

2007	Contemporary Slovak Glass, Leo Kaplan Modern Gallery, New York, USA
2005	Thinking in Glass. Václav Cigler and His School, Gemeentemuseum, The Hague, NL
2003	Masterworks from the Collection of SNG, Slovak National Gallery, Bratislava, SK
2001	Czech Studio Glass, Tai Pei, Taiwan
2000	20th Century, SNG, Slovak National Gallery, Bratislava, SK
	Glass 1989-2000, Lausanne, CH
1999	Action, Word, Space, Municipal Library, Prague, CZ
1998	Castle Klenová, Klatovy, CZ
	Chateau Beychevelle, Bordeaux, F
1996	From Light Glass. Contemporary Glass from the Czech Republic, American Craft Museum, New York, USA

Representation in public collections (selection):

Stedelijk Museum, Amsterdam, NL
Kunstgewerbemuseum, Berlin, D
Museum of M. Dobeš, Bratislava, SK
Slovak National Gallery, Bratislava, SK
Moravian Gallery, Brno, CZ
Museum Coburg, Coburg, D
The Corning Museum of Glass, Corning (NY), USA
Musée des Arts Décoratifs, Paris, F
National Gallery, Prague, CZ
Uměleckoprůmyslové muzeum, Prague, CZ
Museum Boljmans Van Beuningen, Rotterdam, NL
Gallery NOVA, Bratislava, SK

CONE, 1999

HALF EGGS, 2003   ↑ **TWO SPHERICAL LENSES,** 2003 (Jonker – Zaremba collection, NL)

Eva Fišerová

1947, Žilina, SK

Glass objects of Eva Fišerová are astonishing pieces that let glass matter speak for itself. The glass objects resemble lumps of crystal-like minerals of different colours. The irregular and rough shapes of the objects combined with smooth polished surfaces are loaded with energy and inner beauty.

1962 – 1966   Secondary School of Glass, Lednické Rovne, SK
1967 – 1973   Academy of Fine Arts and Design, Bratislava, SK
               Department of Glass in Architecture (V. Cigler)

Solo Exhibitions (selection):
2008   Imagination, Zoya Gallery, Bratislava, SK
2005   Lumen Mundi, Slovak Institute, Budapest, H
               Fascinations, Poprad, SK
2004   Vision, Gallery at Jánsky Hill, Prague, CZ
2001   Gallery NOVA, Bratislava, SK
1999   Vision, Municipal Gallery, Bratislava, SK
               Inspiration, Gallery Léclat du Verre, Paris, F
               Vision, Studio Glass Gallery, London, UK
1997   Les sculptures de verre Eva Fišerová, Wacken, Gallery Nadir, Strassbourg, F

Group Exhibitions (selection):
2006   Sculpture and Object, Bratislava, SK
2005   Faymoreau – Expressions D'Art, Musée du Centre Minier de Faymoreau, F
               Municipal museum, The Hague, NL
2004   Lumen Mundi Eva Fišerová and Jozef Jankovič, Gallery Divyd, Bratislava, SK
2001   SOFA, Chicago, Gallery at Jánsky Hill, USA
1999   SOFA, New York, USA
1998   International glass sculpture, Chateau Beyschevelle, F
               Slovak art, Collection of Mr. John G. Kelcey, London, UK

Representation in public collections (selection):
Slovak National Gallery, Bratislava, SK
Nationale Nederlanden, Rotterdam, NL
UMPRUM, Prague, CZ
Moravian Gallery, Brno, CZ
Musée des Beaux arts des Rouen, Rouen, F
Galerie Nadir, Annecy, F

ANIMA CANDIDA, *1999*

CONJUNCTION, 1993

PLASMA OBJECT

KRABAK, 1997   ↑ ALTERNATIVE, 1992

J u r a j   G a v u l a

1942, Vyšné Čabiny, SK

Juraj Gavula has followed a journey of investigating different materials such as stone, wood, metal and glass in his art works. His early works were marked by Cigler's teaching and were characterized by purity of line and shape, and reduced colour. However, organic shapes of these objects were suggesting an escape from geometry. His glass objects used the expressive properties of melted glass, colour, and rough surfaces. Above all, the combinations of glass with materials of completely different properties result in tension between fragile and solid, transparent and opaque, colour and colourless.

1959 – 1963	Secondary School of Applied Arts, Bratislava, SK
1963 – 1969	Academy of Fine Arts and Design, Bratislava, SK
	Department of Glass in Architecture (V. Cigler)
1990 – 2007	Head of the Department of Glass Design,
	Academy of Fine Arts and Design, SK

Solo Exhibitions (selection):

1998	Gallery NOVA, Bratislava, SK
1993	Museum of Modern Art of the Family Warhol, Medzilaborce, SK
1992	Museum of Ukrainian Culture, Svidník, SK

Group Exhibitions (selection):

2007	Department of Glass Design 1990 – 2007,
	Gallery of M. A. Bazovský, Trenčín, SK
2005	Department of Glass, Gallery Čadca, SK
1999	Transparence, Catsle La Roche, Gyon, F
	Glass Reflections, Municipal Gallery, Bratislava, SK
1998	Glass Sculpture and Object, Expo 98, Lisbon, P
1997	30th Anniversary of the Department of Glass Design,
	Gallery of M. A. Bazovský, Trenčín, SK
	Orava Gallery, Dolný Kubín, SK
1996	Glasskunst Triennale, Norimberg, D
	Slovak Glass, Strasburg, F

Representation in public collections (selection):

Slovak National Gallery, Bratislava, SK
East-Slovak Gallery, Košice, SK
Šariš Gallery, Prešov, SK
Museum of Ukrainian Culture, Svidník, SK

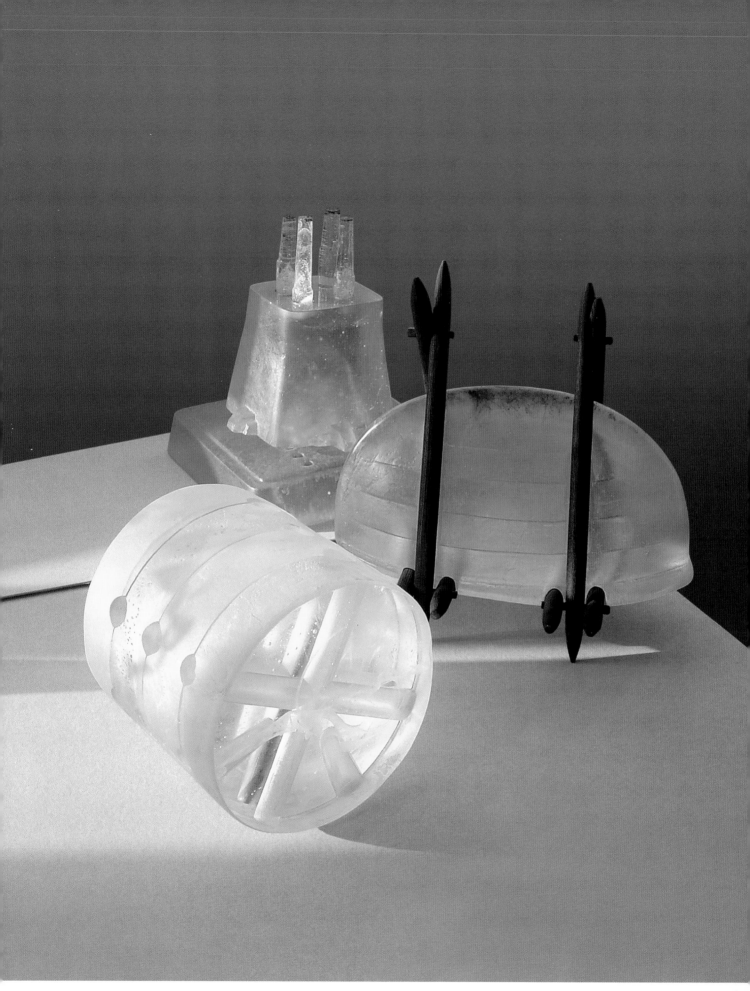

INTERNAL SPACE, 2000

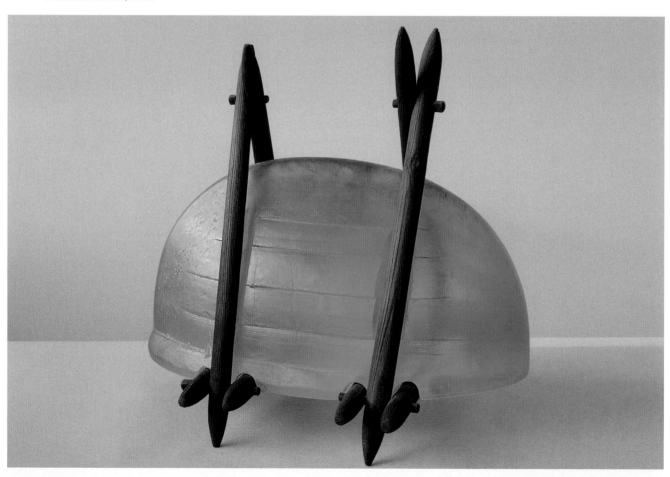

OBJECT, 2000

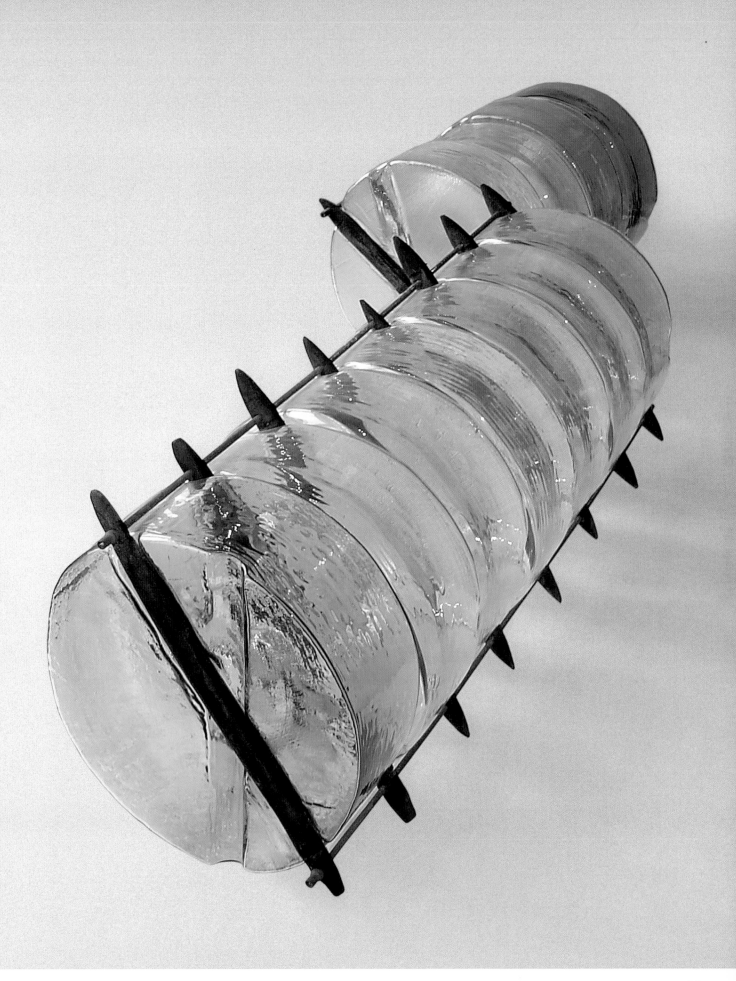

Ašot Haas

1981, Moscow, RUS

Ašot Haas is the winner of the first edition of the Gallery NOVA Award – Glass 2007. Innovative exploration of new dimensions in glass matter in combination with other materials, application of novel technologies for processing glass, creativity and precise execution of his art-works characterise the work of this young artist. He follows the geometric stream by applying the constructivist and minimalist tendencies. He sparked attention with geometric-like objects immersed in glass which he created by placing small metal particles in between sheets of glass and/or using metal foil. The form of the immersed objects is ambiguous as it changes due to viewer's motion.

1996 – 2000   Secondary School of Applied Arts, Bratislava, SK
                      Department of Sculpture (V. Pohanka)
2000 – 2007   Academy of Fine Arts and Design, Bratislava, SK
                      Department of Sculpture (J. Meliš)

Solo Exhibition:
2007   Gallery NOVA, Bratislava, SK

Group Exhibitions:
2007   Finalists of Gallery NOVA Award Glass 2007, Gallery Z, Bratislava, SK
                      Gallery NOVA, Bratislava, SK
                      Graduates from the Academy of Fine Arts and Design 07,
                      House of Art, Bratislava, SK
                      St'Art, Gallery NOVA, Strasbourg, F

Representation in public collection:
Gallery NOVA, Bratislava, SK

STRUCTURE, 2007

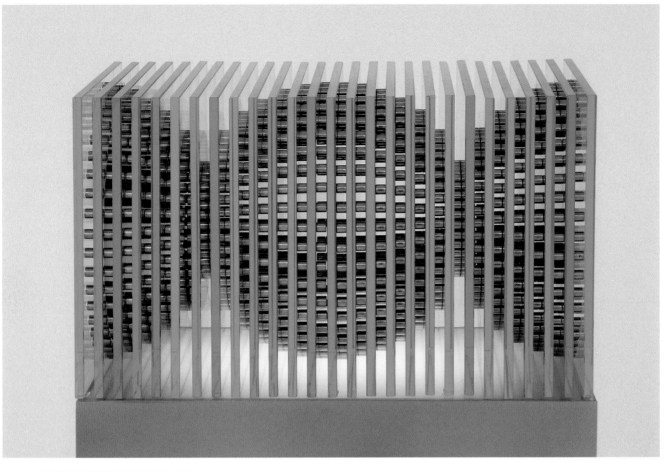

OBJECT WITHIN OBJECT II., 2006

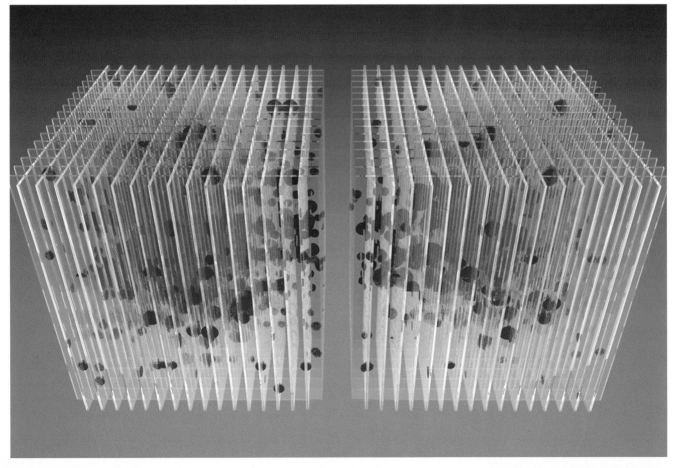

VIRUS, 2008

Pavol Hlôška

1953, Banská Štiavnica, SK

Pavol Hlôška belongs to the followers of the sober geometry of the Cigler School and continues to investigate the inner space of the glass object. He employs the properties of optical glass and the effect of vacuum metallisation of individual glass pieces which form the final object. The pieces are glued together, and the outer surfaces of the object are then polished or given a matt finish. His favoured shapes are sober geometrical forms, such as a prism and lenses. The inner space is fractured into countless variations by the employment of metal patterns. Reflections at these metal patterns depend on the movement of the viewer resulting in the virtual motion of the inner space. The glass objects of Pavol Hlôška spark interest and curiosity. The combination of the object's shape, the glass colour, multiple metal patterns and random light leads to a spectacular experience.

1969 – 1973	Secondary School of Applied Arts, Department of Ceramic, SK
1973 – 1979	Academy of Fine Arts and Design, Bratislava, SK
	Department of Glass in Architecture, (V. Cigler)
1993 – 94	President of Slovak Glass Artists Association
1999	President of Slovak Glass Artists Association

Solo Exhibitions (selection):

2006	Gallery NOVA, Bratislava, SK
2002	Etienne & van den Doel Gallery, The Hague, NL
	Plateaux Gallery, London, UK
2000	Etienne & van den Doel Gallery, The Hague, NL
1998	Galerie Rob van den Doel Gallery, The Hague, NL

Group exhibitions (selection):

2007	Contemporary Slovak Glass, Leo Kaplan Modern Gallery, New York, USA
2006	Coburg Glass Price, Kunstsammlungen der Veste Coburg, Coburg, D
2005	Thinking in Glass, Václav Cigler and His School, Gemeentemuseum, The Hague, NL
	Optical bedroog, Groll Gallery, Naarden, NL
2004	Slovak Glass, Plateaux Gallery, London, UK
	Boulvard des Sculptures, Kijkduin, The Hague, NL
2003	Václav Cigler and his Alumni 1965 – 1979, Mánes, Prague, CZ; MK, SR Bratislava, SK
	PAN Amsterdam, Etienne & van den Doel, Amsterdam, NL
2001	Fasets of Slovak Abstraktion, GALERIE MONTCALM, VilleHull, CAN
	Dialogo con la luce, Galleria "Via Larga", Florence, Roma, IT

Representation in public collections (selection):

Slovak National Gallery, Bratislava, SK
Nationale Nederlanden, Rotterdam, NL
Museum Jan van den Togt, Amstelveen, NL
Kunstsammlungen der Veste Coburg, Coburg, D
Gallery NOVA, Bratislava, SK

OBJECT, 1993 (Jonker – Zaremba collection, NL)

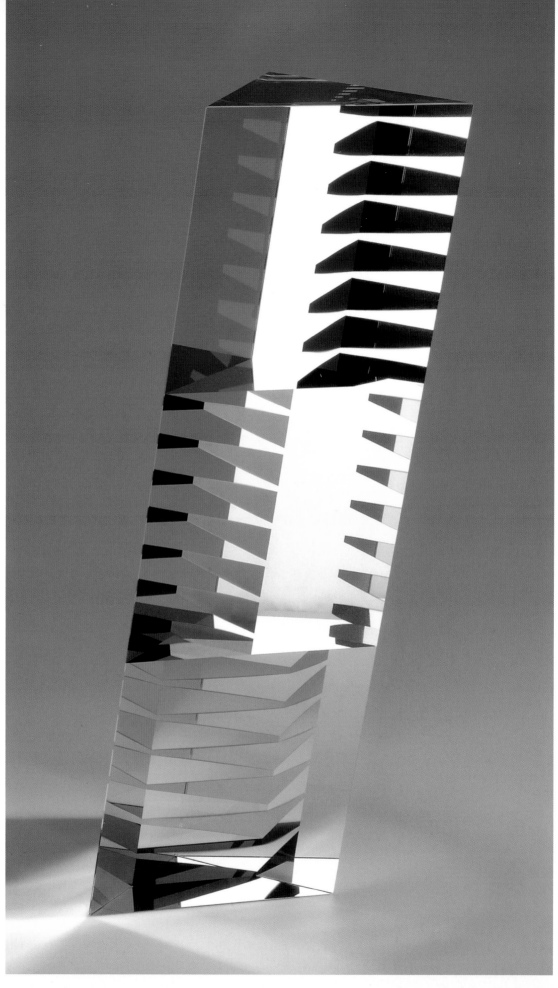

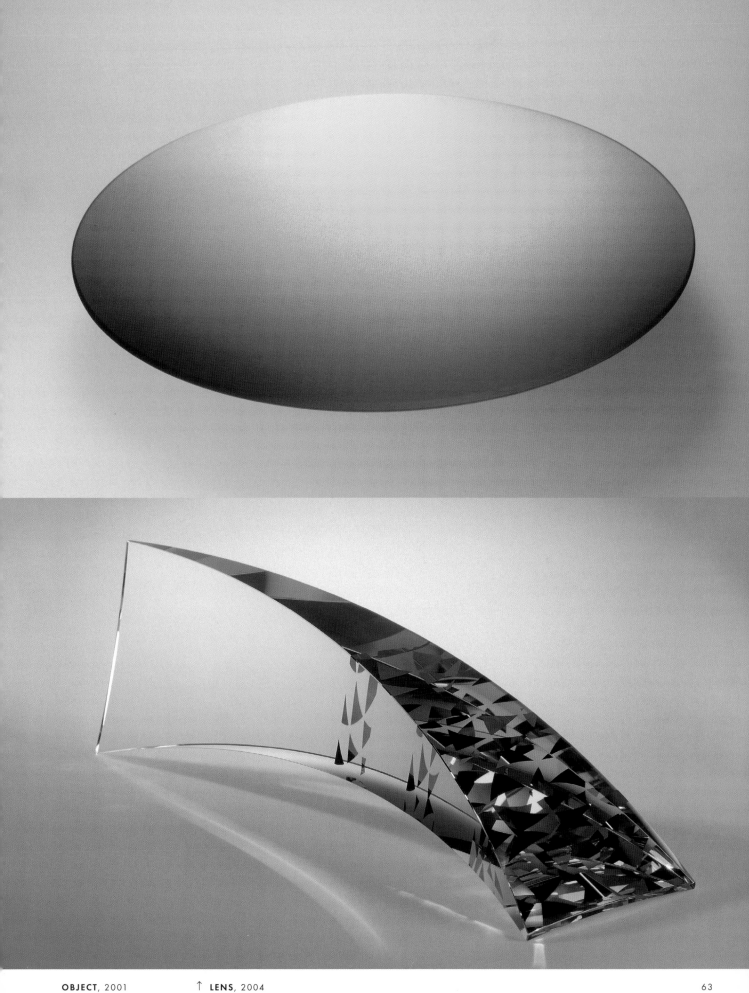

Patrik Illo

1973, Považská Bystrica, SK

The work of Patrik Illo escapes the traditional orientation towards free glass creation. Above all, Illo is a designer. Glass is the material that permits him to create a perfect shape for an applied-art object. His designs follow the traditional form or can be of a completely innovative shape, containing a new witty and playful detail enriching the traditional form. Illo's objects are more than a part of interior; they catch the eyes of the viewer who unconsciously feel their mood-forming presence. The shapes of the objects convey allegories and the viewer is free to change their arrangement to create a new mood. Important are also his glass sculptures and installations that reflect conceptual and minimalist approaches.

1988 – 1992	Secondary School of Applied Arts of Glass, Lednické Rovne, SK
1992 – 1998	Academy of Fine Arts and Design, Bratislava, SK
	Department of Glass Design (J. Gavula)
	Department of Painting, (J. Čarný)
1997	University of Newcastle, UK
1999	Cité Internationale des Arts, Paris, F

Solo Exhibitions (selection):

2007	Gallery NOVA, Bratislava, SK
2006	My Love is Dead, Gallery OELFRUH, Hamburg, D
	Black and White, K Gallery, Bratislava, SK
2005	Pre(D) Woo, (together with M. Škripeň)
	Gallery Belda, Prague, CZ
2004	Gallery Divyd, (together with I. Csudai), Bratislava, SK
	Fragile design by Patrik Illo, Orava Gallery, Dolný Kubín, SK
2001	FOR SALE, (with P. Macho), K Gallery, Bratislava, SK

Group Exhibitions (selection):

2007	Oskar Čepán Award, Gallery Médium, Bratislava, SK
2006	Designmatch, National Gallery, Prague, CZ
	Free Style, Bienale design Saint-Etienne, F
2005	Disorientation, Globe City Gallery, Newcastle upon Tyne, UK
2002	Contemporary Slovak Glass, Slovak Institute, Berlin, D
2001	Galéria via larga, Florence, I
2000	Back to Museum, SNG, Bratislava, SK
1999	Glass?!, Umelecká beseda Slovenska, Bratislava, SK

Representation in public collections (selection):

Slovak National Gallery, Bratislava, SK
Museum of Applied Arts, Prague, CZ
Orava Gallery, Dolný Kubín, SK
Glass Museum, Lednické Rovne, SK
Gallery Oel-Fruh, Hamburg, D

OBJECT, *2007*

KOKTAILLO, *2006*   **KOKTAILLO – WHITE**, *2006*

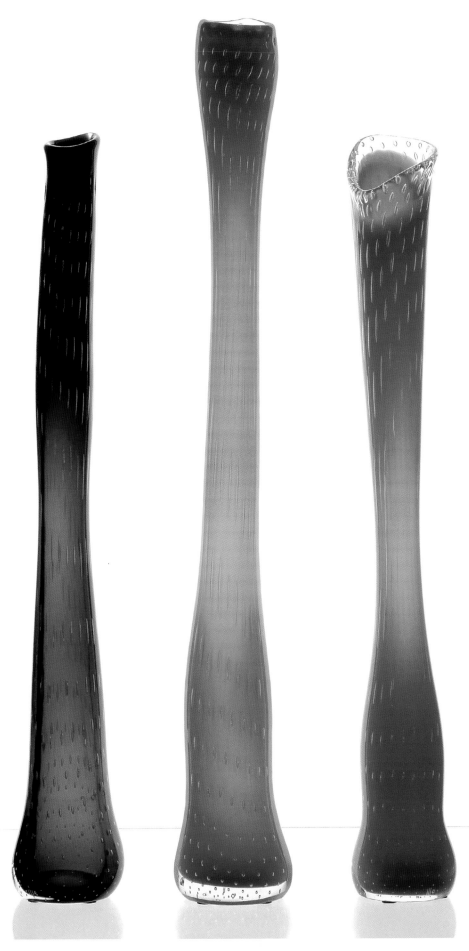

KOKTAILLO – VASES, 2007

Andrej Jakab

1950, Bratislava, SK

Absolute, even sterile geometrical sobriety appears in the works of Andrej Jakab. His objects are simple geometrical structures that get the boost from a concave segment of sphere or a colour veil formed inside the glass matter. The objects of Jakab are admired for their perfect execution and magic inner spaces.

1965 – 1969   Secondary School of Electro Engineering, Bratislava, SK
1969 – 1974   Optika, Bratislava, SK

Solo Exhibitions (selection):
2007   Etienne and van den Doel Gallery, The Hague, NL
2002   Gallery Rob van den Doel Gallery, The Hague, NL
1999   Gallery Ars Temporis, Klagenfurt, A
                Gallery NOVA, Bratislava, SK
1997   Gallery Rob van den Doel Gallery, The Hague, NL
1996   Art Glass Centre Schalkwijk, NL

Group Exhibitions (selection):
2003   Art Point Gallery, Vienna, A
1998   The Verdy Gallery, Mystery of Discovered Space, Sunderland, UK
1996   Studio Glass Gallery London, UK
1994   Espace_94, Nancy, F
1990   Art Show_90, Chicago, USA

Representation in public collections (selection):
Corning Museum, N.Y., USA
NGB, Gouda, NL

BIRD, 2007

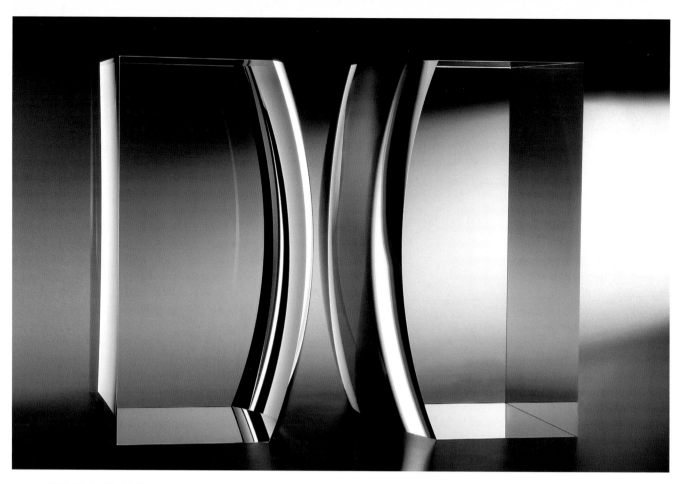

FACE TO FACE, 2007

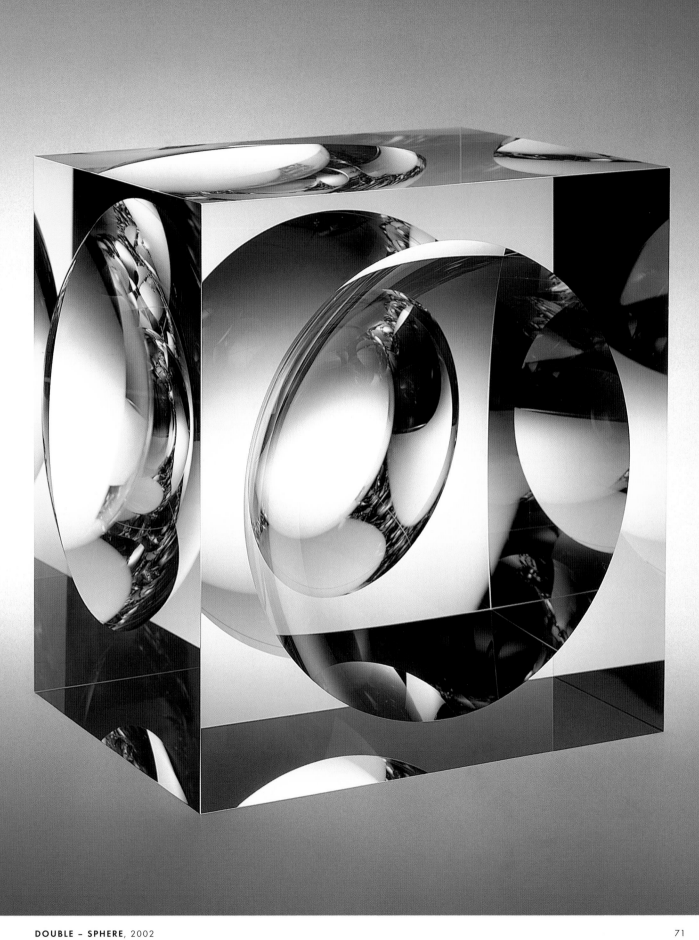

Oliver Leššo

1973, Bratislava, SK

Leššo's objects are masterpieces in providing the viewer with dynamic and fascinating changes of the inner spaces. Oliver Leššo draws inspiration from examples of the older established artists; from their use of simple basic shapes. These are hemispheres, prisms, and discs. The inner structure of the objects is important to him and therefore he rarely disrupts their surfaces and outline. The inner structure is shaped during the very process of the creation of objects, when small regular glass pieces are melted together. The boundaries between the pieces form a structure of a grid or a net that becomes visible in the bulk.

1987 – 1991   Secondary School of Applied Arts, Bratislava, SK
1993 – 1999   Academy of Fine Arts and Design, Bratislava, SK
                Department of Glass Design (J. Gavula)

Solo Exhibitions (selection):
2005   Oliver Leššo, Gallery NOVA, Bratislava, SK
2003   J. – C. Chapelotte Gallery, L
         Gallery SPP, Bratislava, SK
2001   Etienne & Van Den Doel Gallery, The Hague, NL
2000   Gallery Plateaux, London, UK
         Gallery Groll, Naarden, NL

Group Exhibitions (selection):
2007   Gallery NOVA Glass Award, Gallery Z, Bratislava, SK
2006   SOFA Chicago, Plateaux Gallery, USA
2004   Collect, Victoria and Albert Museum, London, UK
         Slovak Glass, Gallery Plateaux, London, UK
2002   Maison du Verre, Puy-Guiliamme, F
2001   Galeria Via Large, Florenc, I
2000   Metamorphosis, Gallery of M. A. Bazovský, Trenčín, Orava Gallery, Dolný Kubín, SK
         Galerie Groll, Naarden, NL

Representation in public collections:
Gallery NOVA, Bratislava, SK

SECRET EYES – RED, 2008

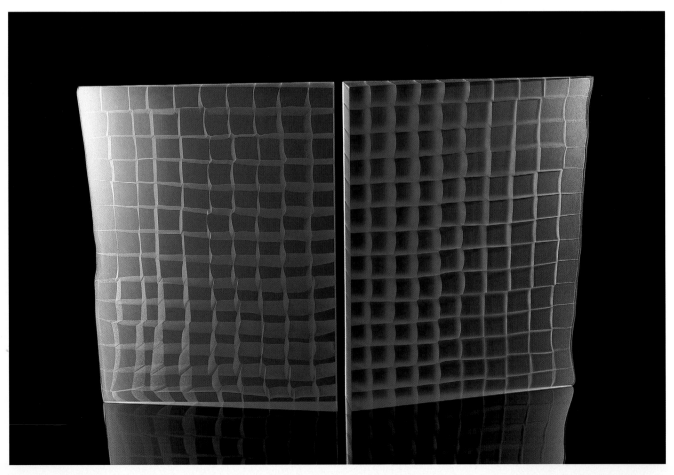

SECRET STRUCTURE – WINGS, 2000

ICE STRUCTURE, 1998

Palo Macho

1965, Streženice, SK

Paľo Macho is a distinctive artist who uses the technique of hot-shaped sheet glass combined with painting on glass. The important elements in his works are a surface texture, colour, and a painting gesture. His works are objects and paintings at the same time and demonstrate the artist's close relationship to contemporary visual art. Macho applies abstract, geometric painting which has a strong lyrical effect. His objects are not decorative paintings; they absorb the viewer into their own space and invite for contemplation.

1980 – 1983	Secondary School of Applied Arts of Glass, Nový Bor, CZ
1983 – 1986	Secondary School of Applied Arts of Glass, Kamenický Šenov, CZ
1989 – 1995	Academy of Fine Arts and Design, Bratislava, SK
	Department of Glass Design (J. Gavula)
1993	École des Beux Artes, Paris, F
1997	Cité Internationale des Artes, Paris, F

Solo exhibitions (selection):

2007	IN EXTENSO, Orava Gallery, Dolný Kubín, SK
	Finnish Glass Museum, Riihimäki, FIN
2005	Tranzit workshop, Bratislava, SK
	Power and Meaning, Gallery SPP, Bratislava, Prešov, SK
2004	Painting ? Painting !, Gallery SPP, Bratislava, SK
2003	New Pictures, Gallery NOVA, Bratislava, SK
	Forms and faces, Budapest, H
	For sale, K-Gallery, Bratislava, SK
2001	Flames of my Memory, Etienne & Van den Doel Gallery, The Hague, NL
	Solve Pingeque, Orava Gallery, Dolný Kubín, SK

Group exhibitions (selection):

2006	Coburg Glass Prize, Coburg, D
2003	Art Glass Society Conference, Global Art Venue, Seattle, USA
2002	Glasstriennial, Märsta, S
	Hadeland Glassverk, Jevnaker, N
2000	Vessels, Koganezaki Glass Museum, JAP
1998	Imagination or Reality, Galerie Cachet, Vienna, A
1997	Slovak Art-Glass, Gallery Rob Van den Doel, The Hague, NL
1995	Glass Now 17, Shizuoka, J

Representation in public collections (selection):

Orava Gallery, Dolný Kubín, SK
Finish Museum of Glass, Riihimäki, FIN

PLANETS (RELIEF), 2005

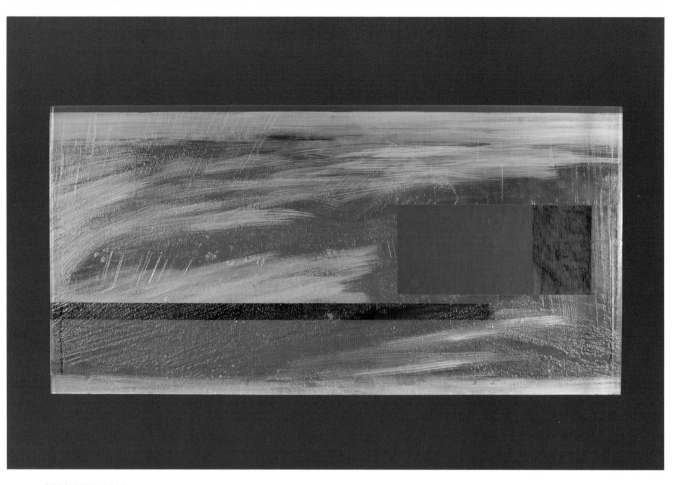

GEOMETRY, 2006

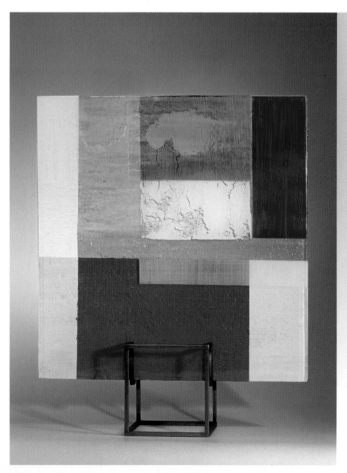

GEOMETRY, 2007

GEOMETRY, 2007

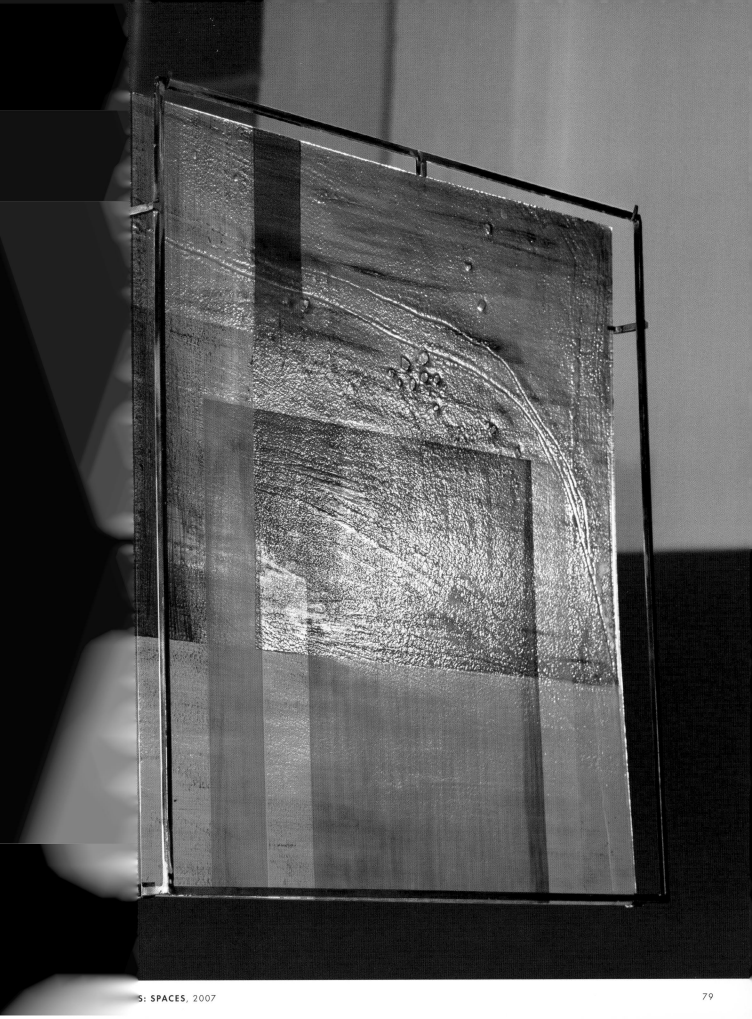

Lukáš Mjartan

1975, Bratislava, SK

The work of Lukáš Mjartan contains a direct influence of the studio of Zora Palová.
Mjartan employs glass with an intense colour. His forms are simple, compact, and
with a self-contained outline. The objects of Mjartan balance between peace and
tension that is achieved by combining thick and thin areas and by contrasting
smooth and rough surfaces. The glass matter is shaped into geometrical patterns.
The geometrical patterns appear like symbols of mankind cast into the material that
is known and used through out its history.

1994 – 2000	Academy of Fine Arts and Design in Bratislava, SK
	Department of Industrial Design (F. Burian)
1997	University of Fine Arts Krakow, PL
1998	University of Sunderland, UK
	Department of Glass, Architectural glass, and Ceramics
2004	University of Sunderland, UK
	Department of Glass, Architectural glass and Ceramics, artist in residence

Solo Exhibitions:

2006	Gallery NOVA, Bratislava, SK
2003	J. – C. Chapellote Gallery, Luxembourg, L

Group exhibitions:

2008	Gallery M. P. Visser, 's-Hertogenbosch, NL
	SOFA 2008, Chicago, USA
	4th Anniversary Invitational, Prism Contemporary Glass, Chicago, USA
2007	Leo Kaplan Modern Gallery, New York, USA
	St'Art, Gallery NOVA, Strasbourg, F
2006	Maiden Lane Exhibition Space, New York, USA
	St'Art, Gallery NOVA, Strasbourg, F
	Coburg Glass Prize for Contemporary Glass in Europe 2006,
	Kunstsammlungen der Veste Coburg, Coburg, D

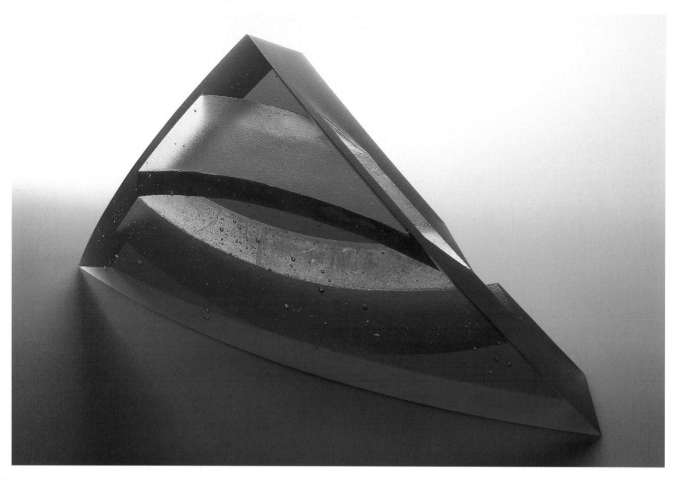

PROVIDENCE, 2006

ZEPHIROS, 2007

Tomáš Ondroušek

1985, Bratislava, SK

The art-works of Tomáš Ondroušek demonstrate his creativity potential, excellent mastery and contemplation in glass. He explores the expressive possibilities of glass by combining it with other materials. It is not the aesthetic effect of glass but, on the contrary, its expressive qualities that stand in the focus of Ondroušek's interest. In the objects that represent bombs with a mysterious content he integrates technical parts into glass cases. Mechanical mechanisms and light sources are placed inside the cases that illuminate and animate the glass matter.

2000 – 2004	Secondary School of Applied Arts of J. Vydra, Bratislava, SK
Since 2005	Academy of Fine Arts, Bratislava, SK
	Department of Glass Design (J. Gavula, V. Oravec)

Group Exhibitions:

2008	Gallery M. P. Visser, 's-Hertogenbosch, NL
2007	Finalists of Gallery NOVA Award Glass 2007, Galéria Z, Bratislava, SK
	Department of Glass, Považská Gallery, Trenčín, SK
	St'Art, Gallery NOVA, Strasbourg, F
2008	Departmentt of Glass, Gallery NOVA, Bratislava, SK
	Talente, Gallery X, Bratislava, SK

AIM OF LIFE II., 2007

AIM OF LIFE III., 2007

Milan Opalka

1961, Žilina, SK

Glass objects of Milan Opalka are intriguing compositions of two disc- or lens-like
objects of contrasting colours. Although one object is transparent and the other of
an intensive colour, usually red, the compositions are aimed to achieve harmony.
Opalka plays with the glass matter and incorporates traces of colour glass into the
pure transparent glass matter to achieve lyrical optical effects.

1976 – 1980	Secondary School of Applied Arts, Bratislava, SK
1980 – 1986	Academy of Fine Arts and Design, Bratislava, SK
	Department of Glass Design (A. Žačko)
Since 1987	active at the Department of Glass Design,
	Academy of Fine Arts and Design, Bratislava, SK.

Solo Exhibitions (selection):

2004	Glass, Turiec Gallery, Martin, SK
	Two in One (together with O. Leššo), Gallery of M. A. Bazovský, Trenčín, SK
2003	Milan Opalka, Unibanka, Bratislava, SK
1991	Milan Opalka-Vetro, Municipio Motta di Livenza, Trevizo, I

Group Exhibitions (selection):

2007	Finalists of Gallery NOVA Glass Award, Gallery Z, Bratislava, SK
2006	Coburger Glasspreis Coburg, D
2003	Cont art, Gallery of City Krakow, PL
2002	Galerie Groll, Naarden, NL
	Alliance – Interference, House of Art, Bratislava, SK
2000	Plateaux Gallery, London, UK

Representation in public collections (selection):

Motto di Livenza, Trevizo, I

ROADS, 2002

DOWNFALL – ICARUS, 2004

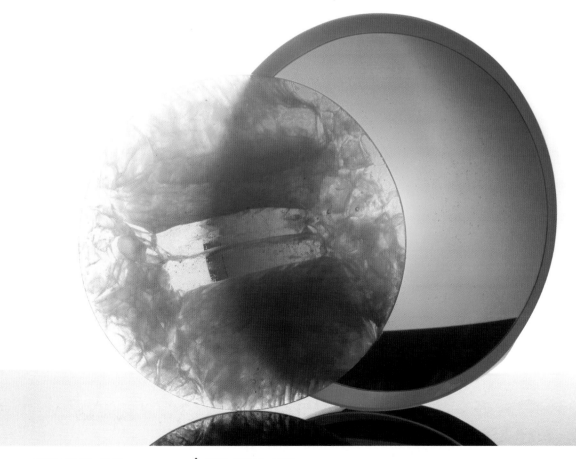

TWO OF US, 2006   ↑ FALL ANGEL, 2001

Juraj Opršal

1953, Martin, SK

The objects of Juraj Opršal are strictly geometrical objects. He takes full advantage of the properties of the optical glass to create objects and compositions with elegance and cold beauty.

1968 – 1972	Secondary School of Applied Arts, Kremnica, SK
1972 – 1978	Academy of Fine Arts and Design, Bratislava, SK
	Department of Glass in Architecture (V. Cigler)
Since 2005	Academy of Fine Arts and Design in Bratislava, SK

Solo Exhibitions (selection):

2003	Gallery Komart, Bratislava, SK
2000	Umelecká beseda slovenská, Bratislava, SK
	Galerie Rob van der Doel, The Hague, NL
1994	The Studio Gallery, London, UK
1993	Gallery Suzy Gottschalk-Bety, Paris, F

Group Exhibitions (selection):

2004	Oisterwijk Sculpture, Oisterwijk, NL
	Homage Rob van der Doel, Oisterwijk, NL
2003	Václav Cigler and his Alumni 1965 – 1979, Mánes Prague, CZ; Bratislava, SK
1999	Glass is Life, Glass Museum, Ebeltoft, D
1998	Slovak Glass, Naarden, NL
1997	Glassgalerie Hittfeld, Hittfeld, D
1996	Triennial of Sculpture, Norimberg, D
1995	Slovak Glass Sculpture, L

Representation in public collections (selection):

Slovak National Gallery, Bratislava, SK
Glass Museum, Ebeltoft, D
Museé du Verre, Rouen, F
Musem of M. Dobeš, Bratislava, SK
Nationale Netherlanden, Amsterdam, NL
Museum van der Togt, Amstelveen, NL

JULIANSTRAUM, 1994

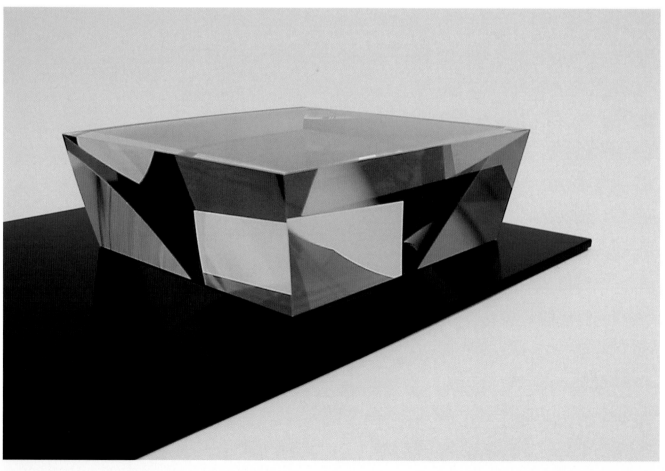

SENTIMENT, 2005

Viktor Oravec

1960, Žilina, SK

Viktor Oravec uses real glass objects as a part of performances and/or to create installations. The glass material helps him to bring attention to events taking place in nature and to human activities.

1975 – 1979	Secondary School of Applied Arts, Bratislava, SK
1979 – 1985	Academy of Fine Arts and Design, Bratislava, SK
	Department of Glass Design (A. Žačko)
Since 2008	Head of Department of Glass Design,
	Academy of Fine Arts and Design, Bratislava, SK

Solo Exhibitions:

2005	22.12.2012, Záhorie Gallery, Senica, SK
2001	Odyssey 2001/PF 2002, Synagogue GJK, Trnava, SK
1995	4 Slovak Artists, (together with M. Pagáč), Santa Barbara, USA
1994	Fragmente, Heiligenkreuzerhof, (together with M. Pagáč), Vienna, A

Group Exhibitions:

2007	From the City, Bratislava City Gallery, Bratislava, SK
2006	Autopoesis, Slovak National Gallery, Bratislava, SK
	Between the Times, Bratislava City Gallery,
	(D. Brunovský, S. Ilavský, V. Oravec, M. Pagáč), Bratislava, SK
2004	Confinium, Záhorie Gallery, Senica, SK
2003	Václav Cigler and his School, Mánes, Prague, CZ
2001	Lighthouse, Považská galéria umenia, Žilina, GJK, Trnava, SK
2000	Body and East, Exit Gallery, New York, USA

Representation in public collections:

Slovak National Gallery, Bratislava, SK

Bratislava City Gallery, Bratislava, SK

1. Slovak Invest Company, Bratislava, SK

OASIS, 2006

BEFORE AND AFTER, 2006

Štepán Pala

1944 Zlín, CZ

The art-works of Štepán Pala are masterpieces that investigate new possibilities in discovering space. Besides being an artist, he is scientist, mathematician, philosopher and alchemist who based his work on the consistent application of mathematics. Geometry is not the eventual target for him; it is simply a means of revealing the hidden spaces of the universe. Pala develops mathematical models and schemes of the world's existence, transforming them into playful structural objects. The glass object is for Štepán Pala more than an object of art – it is a spiritual medium.

1963 – 1967	Secondary School of Applied Arts of Glass, Kamenický Šenov, CZ
1969 – 1975	Academy of Fine Arts and Design, Bratislava, SK
	Department of Glass in Architecture (V. Cigler)
1999 – 2002	Visiting Professor, University of Sunderland, UK

Solo Exhibitions (selection):
2004	Gallery Komart, Bratislava, SK
	Monuments, Zora Palová and Štepán Pala, L
2003	Harmony in Glass, (together with Z. Palová), Zelený dom, Bratislava, SK
2002	Possibilities of Space, Gallery Z, Bratislava, SK
2001	Possibilities of Space, Gallery Pokorná, Prague, CZ
1999	Spaces, Galler at Jánsky Hill, Prague, CZ
	Štěpán Pala, Glass, Habatat Galleries, Florida, USA
1998	Zora Palová and Štepán Pala, Gallery Art du Verre, L
1996	Synergy, The Studio Glass Gallery, London, UK

Group exhibitions (selection):
2007	Berengo Studio, Murano, Venice, I
	Masterworks, Habatat Galleries, Michigan, USA
2006	European neo-constructivism 1930 – 2000, Museum of Contemporary Art, Moscow, RUS
	Coburger Glass Award, Coburg
2005	Thinking in Glass, Václav Cigler and His School, Gemeentemuseum, The Hague, NL
2003	Václav Cigler and his Alumni 1965 – 1979, Mánes, Prague, CZ; Bratislava, SK
2001	Club of Concretizes SK (Homage to Alojz Klimo), Gallery Z, Bratislava, SK
2000	The 20.th Century, Slovak National Gallery, Bratislava, SK

Representation in public collections (selection):
Slovak National Gallery, Bratislava, SK
Museum of Applied Arts, Prague, CZ
Museum of Fine Arts, Kanazawa, J
Collection of Queen of Holland, NL
ING, Rotterdam, NL
V&A Museum, London, UK

CUBES, C. 1995

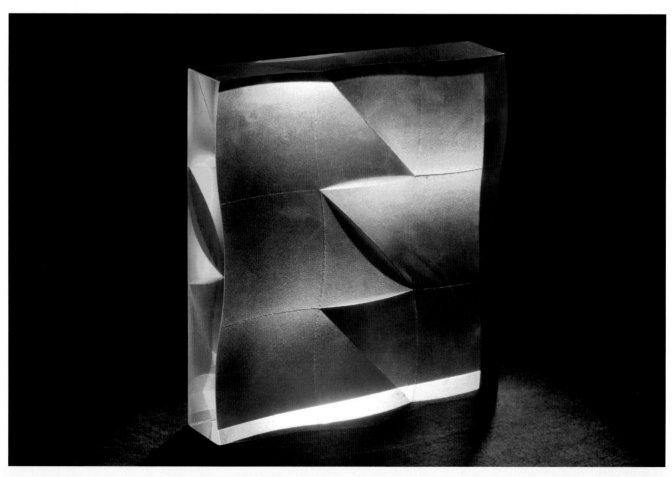

SEA WAY, 2007

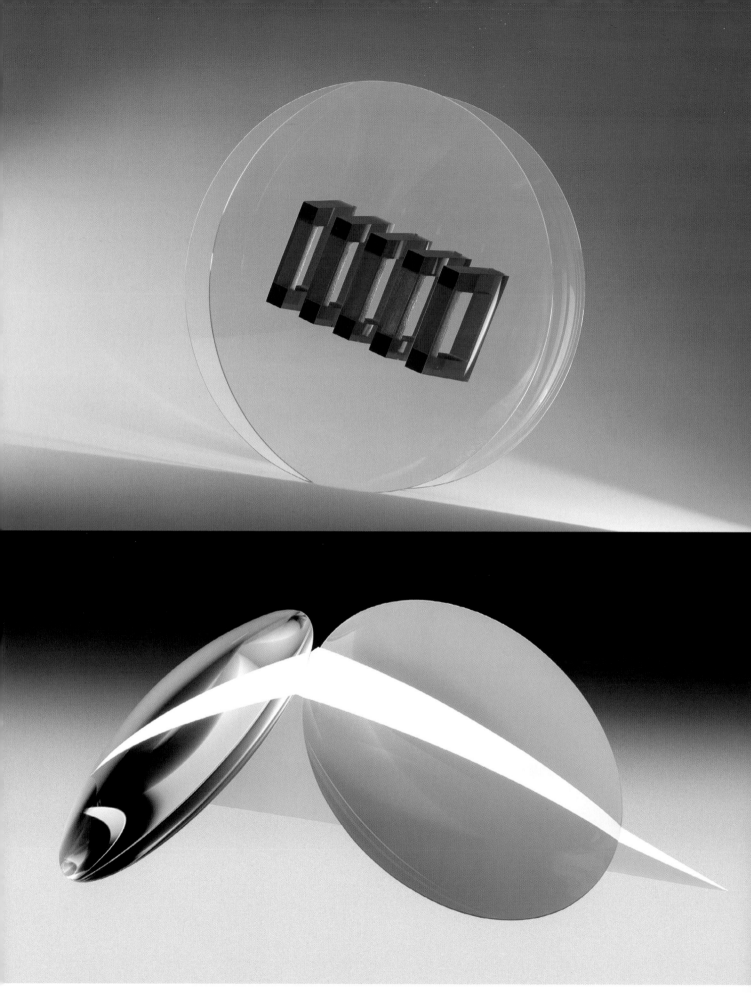

MESSENGER, 1995 ↑ **LIGHT TRANSFORMER**, 1999

Zora Palová

1947, Bratislava, SK

She abandoned the geometry of optical glass, gradually turning towards expressive melted sculpture. The basic building element of her sculptures is color, which becomes the determining means of expression and semantic carrier. Palová prefers intense colors that produce an immediate impression on the spectator. Color fills forms inspired in both nature and man, giving origin to symbols and totems of color and light.

1963 – 1967	Secondary School of Applied Arts, Bratislava, SK
1969 – 1975	Academy of Fine Arts and Design, Bratislava, SK
	Department of Glass in Architecture (V. Cigler)
1996 – 2002	Research professor at the University of Sunderland, UK
Since 2003	Visiting professor at the University of Sunderland, UK

Solo Exhibitions (selection):

2008	Gallery J. – C. Chappelotte, L
2005	Sunderland's Inspirations, Gallery NOVA, Bratislava, SK
2004	Monumentales, Zora Palová and Štepán Pala, Gallery J. – C. Chappelotte, L
2003	Harmony in Glass, (together with Š. Pala), Zelený dom, Bratislava, SK
2002	I am here, Gallery Pokorná, Prague, CZ
2000	Glass Sculptures, Gallery J. – C. Chappelotte, L
1999	Amygdale, Habatat Galleries, Florida, USA
1997	Zora Palová and Štepán Pala, Gallery Art du Verre, L

Group Exhibitions (výber):

2007	Berengo Studio, Murano, Venice, I
	Masterworks, Habatat Galleries, Michigan, USA
	Modern Masters, 59. Internationalen Handwerksmesse, Munich, D
2006	Gallery NOVA, Bratislava, SK
	Coburg Glass Prize for Contemporary Glass in Europe, Coburg, D
2005	Thinking in Glass, Václav Cigler and His School, Gemeentemuseum, The Hague, NL
2003	Vaclav Cigler and his Alumni 1965 – 1979, Mánes, Prague, CZ
2002	Thinking Big, Sculpture at Goodwood, Peggy Gugenheim Collection, Venice, I
2001	Glass Connections, National Glass Centre, Sunderland, UK

Representation in public collections (selection):

Museum of Applied Arts, Prague, CZ
Slovak National Gallery, Bratislava, SK
Nationale Netherlanden, Rotterdam, NL
Shimonoseki Museum of Modern Art, J
Ulster Museum, Belfast, IRL
Victoria & Albert Museum, London, UK
Kunst Sammlungen der Veste Coburg, D

CELL, 2006

ICE LEAF, 1998

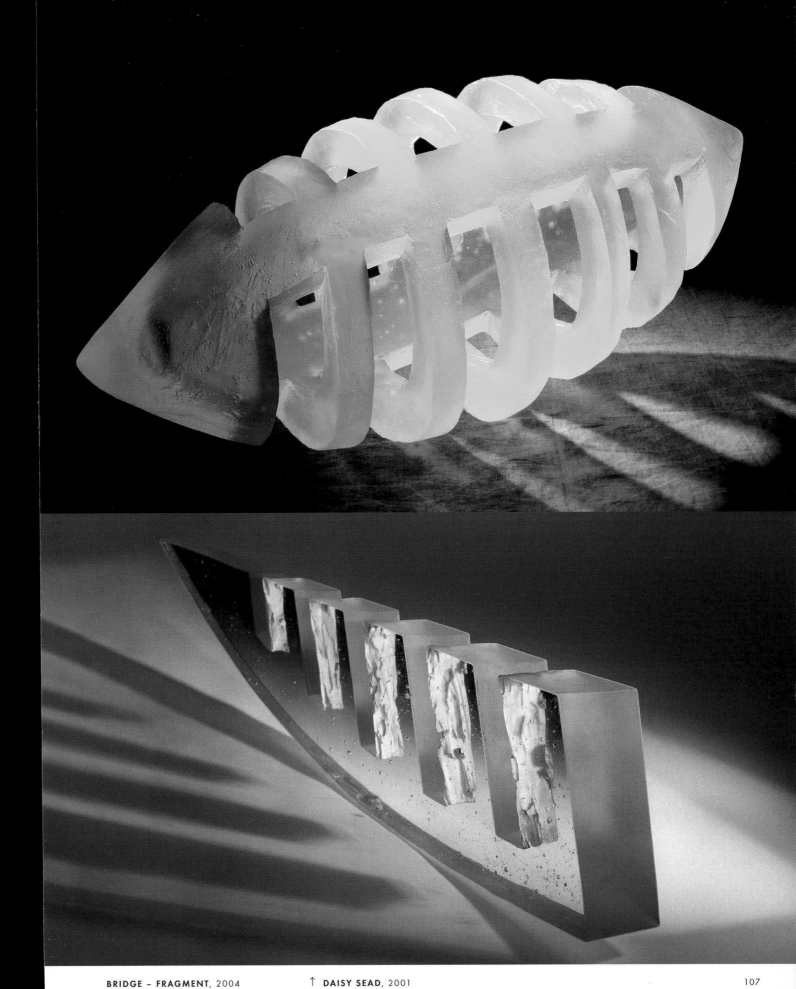

BRIDGE – FRAGMENT, 2004   ↑ DAISY SEAD, 2001

Lenka Šimonyiová

1981, Bratislava, SK

Šimonyiová from the very beginning of her young career works in the way of transparent plate or optical glass. The main factor of her work is geometry. The different layers stand against each other in opposition while the cross-banding remains empty. This creates tension between the matter and the empty. Although the object itself is just insinuated by the layers of glass and the silhouette is not compact, it is clearly defined thanks to strict geometry.

2003 – 2008   Academy of Fine Arts and Design, Bratislava, SK
                        Department of Glass Design (J. Gavula, V. Oravec)

Solo exhibition:
2008   Gallery NOVA, Bratislava, SK

Group exhibtions:
2008   Gallery M. P. Visser, 's-Hertogenbosch, NL
2007   St'Art, Gallery NOVA, Strassbourg, F
                    Studio of Glass J. G., Gallery M. A. Bazovský, Trenčín, SK
                    Finalists of the Gallery NOVA Award Glass 2007, Gallery Z, Bratislava, SK
                    Contemporary Slovak Glass, Leo Kaplan Modern Gallery, New York, USA
2006   A Touch of Slovakia, Mons, B
                    St'Art, Gallery NOVA, Strassbourg, F
                    Contemporary Slovak Glass, Gallery NOVA, Bratislava, SK
                    Contemporary Slovak Glass, Maiden Lane Exhibition Space, New York, USA
2005   Exhibition of the Graduates from the Department of Glass, Kysuce Gallery, Čadca, SK

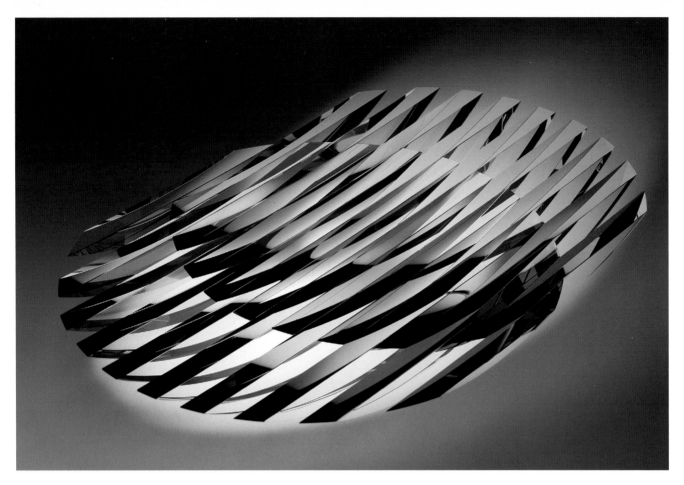

SYMBIOSIS, 2007

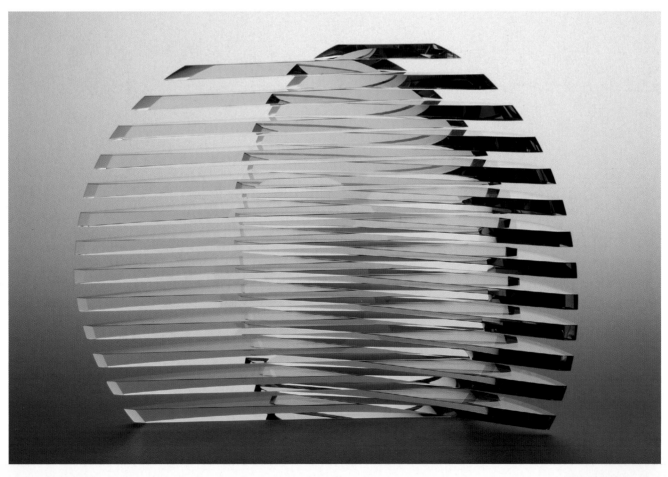

SYMBIOSIS II., 2007

J o z e f   T o m e č k o

1945, Žichovice, CZ

Jozef Tomečko represents the geometrical stream in Slovak glass. He creates objects of fascinating forms of straight or curved outlines, which are results of his search for perfection. He takes full advantage of transparency and reflecting surfaces of the optical glass, and the movement of virtual spaces depending on the position of the viewer.

1959 – 1963	Secondary School of Applied Arts of Glass, Železný Brod, CZ
1966 – 1972	Academy of Fine Arts and Design, Bratislava, SK
	Department of Glass in Architecture (V. Cigler)

Solo Exhibitions (selection):

2003	Gallery Nadir, Annecy, F
1993	Gallery Phídias, Queberon, F
	Glasgalerie, Saarbrücken, D
1992	Gallery Pollack, Montpellier, F
1991	Galerie Internationale du Verre, Biot, F
1989	Gallery Rob van den Doel, The Hague, NL

Group Exhibitions (selection):

2005	Thinking in Glass, Václav Cigler and His School, Gemeentemuseum, The Hague, NL
	Museum Jan van der Togt, Pay-Bas, Amstelveen, NL
2004	French Institute, Bratislava, SK
2003	Václav Cigler and His Alumni 1965 – 1979, Mánes Prague, CZ, Bratislava, SK
	Gallery Nadir, Annency, F
	Atlantic City, USA
	Gallery Klute, Vienna, A
	Gallery Rob van den Doel, The Hague, NL

Representation in public collections (selection):

Slovak National Gallery, Bratislava, SK
Glasmuseum Ebeltoft, Ebeltoft, D
Musée des Arts Décoratifs, Lausanne, CH
Museum of Contemporary Art, Moscow, RUS
Musée de Beaux Arts, Rouen, F
Musée du Verre, Sars Poteries, F

OBJECT, 2003

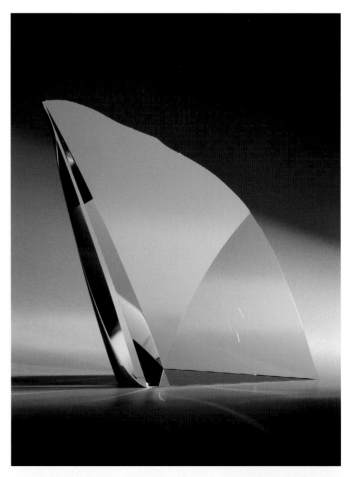

SUMMER BIRD, 2004

Vladimír Zbyňovský

1964, Bratislava, SK

Vladimír Zbyňovský is the artist who knows to breathe in life into glass matter. Zbyňovský lives in France where he has brought his experience from the Department of Glass Design studio at the Academy of Fine Arts and Design in Bratislava. In many respects his work follows the tradition of the Cigler School, above all in his respect to spectacular properties of glass. The peculiarity of his objects is based on the combination of a smooth, viscous, as if molten block of optical glass with a rigid, stationary, and non-transparent stone matter. Glass perfectly emulates the rough surface of the stone. Making use of the optical properties of glass he magnifies the roughness of the stone surface, creating an extraordinary landscape that fascinates the viewer. The landscape within the glass is alive as it changes due to the motion of the viewer.

1980 – 1984	Secondary School of Applied Arts, Bratislava
1985 – 1991	Academy of Fine Arts and Design Bratislava, SK
	Department of Glass Design (A. Žačko, J. Gavula)
1991	Oliver de Serres School of Applied Arts, Paris, F
	He has lived in France since 1993.

Solo Exhibitions (selection):

2005	Etienne & van den Doel Gallery, Oisterwijk, NL
	Rafa'l Goldchain & Vladimir Zbynovsky, "About memory", Galleria Rossella Junck, Berlin, D
2004	Plateaux Gallery, London, UK
2003	Magic, Galerie Terra Viva, St. Quentin la Poterie, F
2000	Galerie Rob van der Doel, The Hague, NL

Group Exhibitions (selection):

2007	Collect, Victoria & Albert Museum, Plateaux Gallery, London, GB
	Verriales, Contraste, Galerie Internationale du Verre, Biot, F
	Czech and Slovak Glass in Exile, Moravian Gallery, Brno, CZ
2006	SOFA New York & Chicago, USA
	Glas Coburg, exposition internationale, Coburg, D
2005	Galerie Internationale du Verre-Serge Lechaczynski, Biot, F
	PAN Amsterdam, Etienne & van den Doel Gallery, The Hague, NL
2004	Eternal light, Spertus Museum, Chicago, USA
2003	Exposition collective de sculptures, Casino du Palm Beach, Cannes, F
2002	Venezia Vetro 2002, Galerie Rossella Junck, Venice, I

Representation in public collections (selection):

Banka de San Paolo, Luxembourg
National Bank of Slovakia, Bratislava, SK
Museum de Meisenthal, F
Museum of Modern Art, Kanazawa, J
Spertus Museum, Chicago, USA
Musée du Verre, Sars-Poterie, F

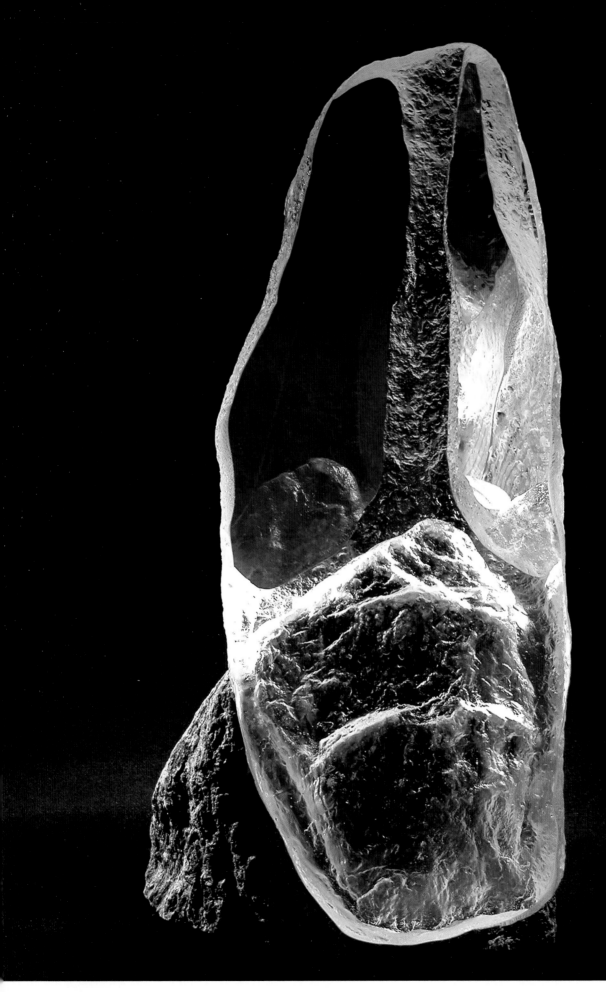

GHOST OF STONE, 2005

GHOST OF STONE, 2007

Ján Zoričák

1944, Ždiar, SK

Some of the specific characteristics of the Bratislava School of Glass are visible also in the work of Jan Zoričák, although he studied in Prague and has lived in France since 1970. His early work reflected the geometry of the Cigler School; however, the Czech glass tradition has been present in his work from the beginning. In France he has become an influential figure in the development and populariza-tion of glass art. His works attract attention by unusual organic forms and intense colours. Zoričák is master in the use of internal structures of glass, such as bubbles and veils, to create fascinating magic world frozen in glass matter.

1959 – 1963   Secondary School of Applied Arts of Glass, Železný Brod, CZ
1963 – 1969   Academy of Applied Arts, Prague, (S. Libenský), CZ

Solo Exhibitions (selection):
2005   Musée du verre, Conche-en-Ouche, F
2003   Municipal Gallery, Mirbach Palace, Bratislava, SK
2002   Gallery Nadir, Lyon, F
              Steninge Slott, Stockholm, S
2001   Glasspyramid Gallery (together with P. Macho, F. Csandal), Budapest, H
              Gallery Daniel Guidat, Cannes, F
              Gallery Place des Arts, Montpellier, F
2000   Gallery l'Eclat du verre, Paris, F
              Gallery Rob van den Doel, The Hague, NL
1997   Slovak National Gallery, Bratislava, SK

Group Exhibitions (selection):
2005   SOFA New York, USA
2003   From fire, The 31st Annual International Glass Invitational, Habatat Galleries,
              Birmingham, USA
2002   The 30th Annual International Glass Invitational, Habatat Galleries, Royal Oak, MI/USA
              Venezia vetro 2002, Spazio Espositivo Rossella Junck, Venice, I
2001   International Glass Symposium 1982 – 2000 Nový Bor, dedicated to S. Libeňský,
              Museum of Applied Arts, Prague, CZ
2000   Contemporary Glass from France, Glass Museum Ebeltoft, Ebeltoft, D
1998   International Exhibition of Glass Kanazawa '98,
              Industrial Gallery of Ishikawa Prefecture, Kanazawa, J

Representation in public collections (selection):
Slovak National Gallery, Bratislava, SK
Toledo Museum of Art, Toledo, USA
Glass Museum, Ebeltoft, DK
Museé des Artes Décoratifs, Paris, F
Kunstsammlungen der Vest, Coburg, D
Mussé du Verre, Sars-Poteries, F

CELESTINE GARDENS, *2006*

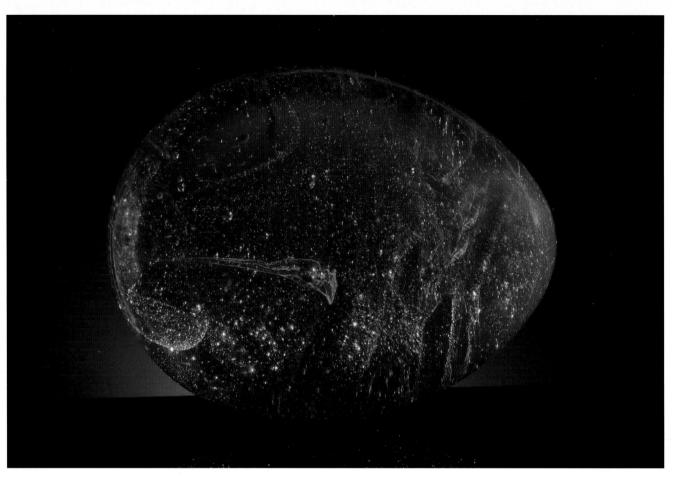

MYSTERY OF LIFE, 1968 – 2006

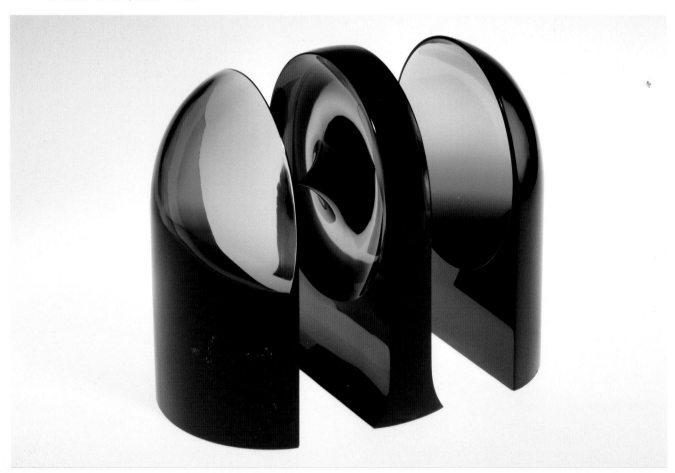

OBJECT, 1971 (Slovak National Gallery)

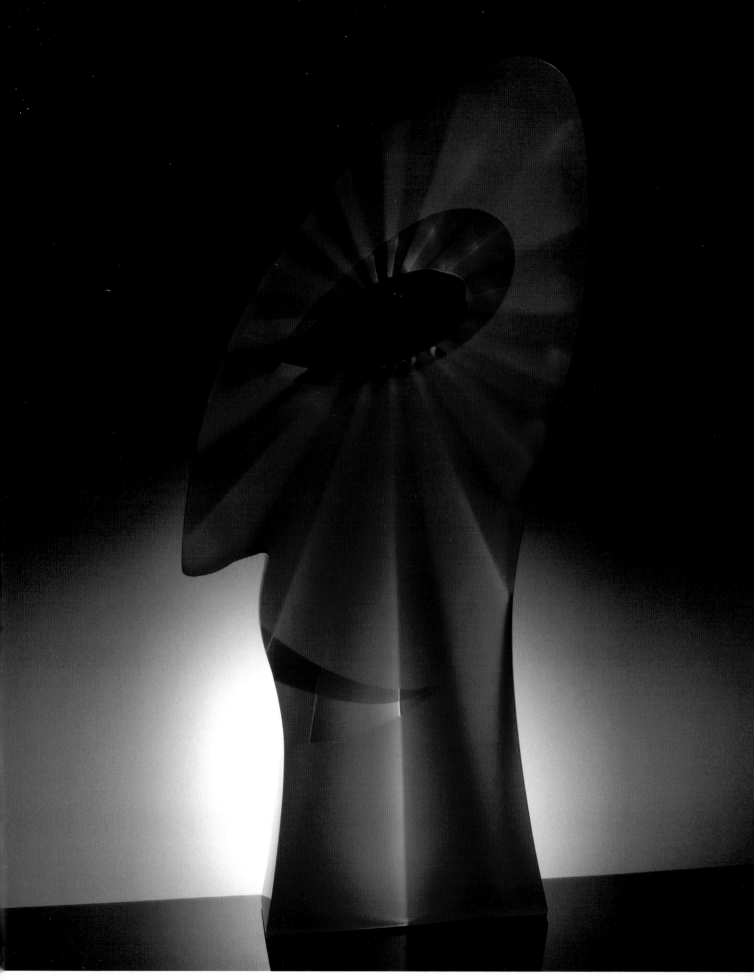

Askold Žačko

1946, Bratislava – 1997, Bratislava, SK

Askold Žačko has an important place in the development of Slovak glass art. He followed Václav Cigler as the head of the Department of Glass Design at Academy of Fine Arts and Design in Bratislava and as a part of education he introduced a wider variety of forms, material combinations, colours and expression. He liberated himself from austere minimalism and geometric sobriety towards more expressive manifestations. Clear transparent objects with symbolic and lyrical themes were gradually replaced by figurative ones using an intense colour. Žačko's objects and sculptures are not idealised, they do not aim to catch the viewer by beauty; they reflect real life by their complexity, tension and aggressiveness.

1960 – 1964	Secondary School of Glass, Železný Brod, CZ
1965 – 1971	Academy of Fine Arts and Design, Bratislava, SK
	Department of Glass in Architecture (V. Cigler)
1979 – 1990	Head of Department of Glass Design at the Academy of Fine Arts
	and Design in Bratislava, SK

Solo Exhibitions (selection):

1997	Galerie Utrecht, Utrecht, NL
1995	Galerie Voutat, Ženeva, CH
1994	Galerie L, Hamburg, D
1993	Essener Glas Galerie, Essen, D
	Miller Gallery, New York, USA
1992	Galerie Hermann, Drachselsried, D
	First Glass Galerie, Munich, D

Group Exhibitions (selection):

2004	Václav Cigler and his Students, Mánes, Prague, CZ; Bratislava, SK
2000	Expression en verre III. Collection du Museé des arts décoratifs, Lausanne, CH
1996	Galerie Élysées Rond-Point, Paris, F
1995	Contemporary Slovak Glass, Lasimuseo, Riihimäki, FIN
	Glas Galerie, Hittfeld, D
1994	Heller Gallery, New York, USA
1992	Briaggotti Gallery, Amsterdam NL
	Mánes, Prague, CZ
1991	Galerie Mitte, Vienna, A

Representation in public collections (selection):

Slovak National Gallery, Bratislava, SK
National Netherlanden, Rotterdam, NL
Samlingen af Moderne International Glaskunst, Ebeltoft, NL
City Bank Corporation, New York, USA
Hermitage, St. Petersburg, RUS

BAROQUE, 1981 (Slovak National Gallery)

BIG CIRCLE, 1996 – 1997 (1. Slovak Invest Company)

DUNE, 1976

Bibliography – Slovak Glass (selected)

ABELOVSKÝ, Ján: Synergie – kresba, catalogue Banská Bystrica 1994

Artist Verriers du Tchécoslovaquie, catalogue, Gallery Transparence, Brussels 1988,
text by A. Adlerová

BAJCUROVÁ, Katarína: Le verre Slovaque. Perspective et réalité.
In: La revue de la céramique et du verre, 1995, No. 84, p. 26 – 30

BAJCUROVÁ, Katarína: Svetelné umenie.
In: Slovník svetového a slovenského výtvarného umenia druhej polovice 20. storočia.
Ed. GERŽOVÁ, Jana. Bratislava, 1999, p. 260 – 265

BAJCUROVÁ, Katarína: Kinetické umenie.
In: Slovník svetového a slovenského výtvarného umenia druhej polovice 20. storočia.
Ed. GERŽOVÁ, Jana. Bratislava, 1999, p. 129 – 131

BAJCUROVÁ, Katarína: A chacun son ciel.
In: La revue de la céramique et du verre, No. 105, 1999, p. 30 – 32

BAJCUROVÁ, Katarína: Art du verre contemporain Slovaque,
In: Mystéres de l'espace, catalogue Maison du Verre de Puy-Guillaume 2002

BAJCUROVÁ, Katarína: Ciglerova "škola myslenia" – včera a dnes.
In: Václav Cigler a absolventi oddelenia sklo v architektúre na Vysokej škole výtvarných umení
v Bratislave 1965 – 1979, 2003

CIGLER, Václav: K výtvarnému programu školy. In: Výtvarný život, 15, 1970, No. 4, p. 13 – 17

CIGLER, Václav: Oddelenie skla v architektúre.
In: VŠVU v Bratislave, 1949 – 1974, Ed. Ľudmila PETERAJOVÁ, Bratislava 1974

Csehszlovák üvegművészet 1945 – 1989, Iparművészeti Múzeum, Budapest 1990

České a slovenské sklo v exile, Moravská galerie, Brno 2007, text S. Petrová

Československé umelecké sklo, catalogue Skloexport Liberec, Munich 1981

Design okolo nás, catalogue Slovenská národná galéria, Bratislava 1980,
text J. Abelovský, A. Osmitzová, A. Žačková

HETTEŠ, Karel: O tradici českého skla a jeho původnosti
In: Czechoslovak Glass Review, 1957, p. 21 – 28

HETTEŠ, Karel: Sklo v Československu, Prague 1958

HETTEŠ, Karel: Glass-making in Slovakia – The History of Its One Thousand Years of Development.
In: Glass Review, 29, 1974, No. 6, p. 8 – 15

HETTEŠ, Karel: Glass-making in Slovakia – The History of Its One Thousand Years of Development.
In: Glass Review, 29, 1974 No. 7, p. 6 – 12

HETTEŠ, Karel: Glass-making in Slovakia – The History of Its One Thousand Years of Development.
In: Glass Review, 29, 1974, No. 8, p. 7 – 10

HETTEŠ, Karel: Glass-making in Slovakia – The History of Its One Thousand Years of Development.
In: Glass Review, 29, 1974, No. 9, p. 5 – 12.

HETTEŠ, Karel: Glass-making in Slovakia – The History of Its One Thousand Years of Development.
In: Glass Review, 29, 1974, No. 10, p. 7 – 14

FORMANKO, Jaroslav: Sklo v optike bilancií. Tridsať rokov bratislavskej sklárskej školy.

In: Literárny týždenník, 10, 1997, No. 3, p. 14

FORMANKO, Jaroslav: Výstava oddelenia sklárskeho výtvarníctva VŠVU v Bratislave

pri príležitosti 30. výročia jeho založenia, Orava Gallery, Dolný Kubín 1997

FORMANKO, Jaroslav: Absolventi a študenti Ateliéru skla doc. Juraja Gavulu

na Vysokej škole výtvarných umení v Bratislave. Čadca 2005

KLEIN, Dan: Odevzdávání vědomostí.

In: Václav Cigler a absolventi Oddelenia skla v architektúre na VŠVU v Bratislave 1965 – 1979,

catalogue, Prague 2003

MEDKOVÁ, J.: Metamorfózy skla, catalogue, Moravian Gallery, Brno 1972

PETROVÁ, Silvie: České sklo. Prague 2002

PETERAJOVÁ, Ľudmila: Vysoká škola výtvarných umení 1979 – 1984, Bratislava 1989

PETERAJOVÁ, Ľudmila: Vysoká škola výtvarných umení v Bratislave, 1949 – 1989.

In: Vysoká škola výtvarných umení 1949 – 1999, Bratislava 1999

RAČEKOVÁ, Jarmila: Súčasné umelecké sklo na Slovensku.

In: Ars, 1977 – 81, No. 1 – 4, p. 140 –173

RAČEKOVÁ, Jarmila: Sklo v monumentálno-dekoratívnej tvorbe na Slovensku v rokoch 1948 – 1973.

In: Ars, 1985, No. 2, p. 67 – 83

RAČEKOVÁ, Jarmila: Contemporary Glass Sculpture in Slovakia, Bratislava 1989

RAČEKOVÁ, Jarmila: Sklená plastika na Slovensku v poslednom dvadsaťročí.

In: Súčasné výtvarné umenie. Ed: SRNENSKÁ Dagmar. Bratislava 1989, p. 1 – 28

RAČEKOVÁ, Jarmila: Lednické Rovne. In: Neue Glasrevue, 1992, No. 11, p. 4 – 7.

RAČEKOVÁ, Jarmila: Lednické Rovne 1994. In: New Glass Review, 1994, No. 11, p. 28 – 29

RAČEKOVÁ, Jarmila: Mystery of Discovered Space. Contemporary Slovak Glass.

In: Neues Glass, 1998, No. 3, p. 32 – 39

Slovenské súčasné užité umenie, Československé kultúrne a informačné stredisko, Cairo 1975,

text by A. Žačková

ŠINDELÁŘ, Dušan: Současné umelecké sklo v Československu, Prague 1970

Thinking in Glass. Václav Cigler and His School, Geementemuseum, Den Haag 2005

TROJANOVÁ, Eva: 3. Internationale Glaskunst Triennale. Catalogue, Nürnberg 1999

TROJANOVÁ, Eva: Dialogo con la luce.

(Cristallo slovacco contemporaneo), catalogue Roma 2001

Verres du Bohéme 1400 – 1989, catalogue, Museé des Art Décoratifs, Paris 1989, text by S.Petrová

ŽAČKOVÁ, Agáta: Súčasné slovenské umelecké sklo a šperk,

Slovak National Gallery, Bratislava 1985

ŽAČKOVÁ, Agáta: History and permanent glass-making in Slovakia.

In: Glassreview, 42, 1987, No. 2, p. 37

ŽAČKOVÁ, Agáta: Súčasné slovenské sklo – Galéria architektúry, užitého umenia a dizajnu,

Slovak National Gallery, Bratislava 1991

The list of the graduates
at the Academy of Fine Arts
and Design in Bratislava.

Department of Glass in Architecture, 1965 – 1979
Head of the department: Václav Cigler

1968 – Jozef Vachálek
1969 – Juraj Gavula, Ivan Polák, Milan Pulík
1971 – Ivan Hrošo, Vladimír Kordoš, Marián Mudroch, Štefan Partl, Askold Žačko
1972 – Ján Lišaník, Josef Tomečko
1973 – Eva Dolejšiová-Fišerová, Pavel Tomečko
1974 – Jiří Boháč
1975 – Štepán Pala
1977 – Karol Drexler, Ladislav Pagáč, Eva Ilkovičová-Potfajová
1978 – Anna Daučíková, Milan Gašpar, Juraj Opršal
1979 – Michal Gavula, Pavol Hlôška, Rudolf Višňovský

Department of Glass Design 1980 – 1990
Head of the department: Askold Žačko

1980 – Mária Horváthová, Tamara Klimová, Jozef Kolembus
1982 – Ján Mýtny
1983 – Mária Hajnová, Juraj Steinhubel
1984 – Miloš Balgavý, Jaroslav Gaňa
1985 – Magda Burmeková, Viktor Oravec
1986 – František Kováč, Milan Opálka
1987 – Daniela Marthová, Drahomír Prihel
1990 – Marta Mlíchová, Milan Richter

Department of Glass Design, 1990 – 2007
Head of the department: Juraj Gavula

1991 – Vladimír Zbyňovský
1992 – Martin Masarovič, Peter Šipoš
1993 – František Csandal, Ján Gabriška
1994 – Vojtech Ferdics, Patrik Kovačovský (Bc)
1995 – Slavomír Bachorík, Luboš Kips (Bc), Pavol Macho, Erika Nielepová (Bc), Ivica Markovičová
1996 – Matej Gavula
1997 – Lucia Hronská (Bc), Peter Ondrušek, Filip Vilhan, Jana Znášiková (Bc)
1998 – Patrik Illo, Žaneta Skybová, Peter Pohanka
1999 – Alexandra Chovancová, Oliver Leššo, Rastislav Sliacky (Bc)
2000 – Andrej Jakab (Bc), Leoš Smejkal (Bc)
2001 – Tamara Bohuňková, Samuel Juriš
2002 – Martin Partl, Anna Učníková (Bc), Barbora Zdravecká
2003 – Peter Miko, Martin Múranica (Bc), Mária Štefančíková (Bc)
2005 – Petra Vlhová-Jureňová
2006 – Marek Brincko
2007 – Mária Berkyová, Mária Drozdová (Bc), Ján Gašparovič, Ján Hanušiak (Bc),
       Jana Ivaničová (Bc), Silvia Mikúšová (Bc), Lenka Šimonyiová (Bc)

Slovak Contemporary Glass

Gallery NOVA

Editor: Katarína Beňová
Foreword: Dan Klein, UK
Texts: Katarína Beňová, Sabina Jankovičová, Miroslav Zeman
Translation: Castor Sanchez, Miroslav Zeman
English text editing: Ruth Steketee-Engledow
Photographs:
Milota Havránková (V. Cigler, M. Balgavý, L. Artz, P. Hlôška, Z. Palová, Š. Pala),
Jana Hojstričová (L. Arzt, M. Balgavý, M. Brincko, V. Cigler,
P. Macho, V. Oravec, M. Tomečko, L. Šimonyiová),
Andrej Jakab jun. (A. Jakab),
Ingrid Patočková (P. Illo),
Valéria Zacharová (L. Mjartan, Š. Pala, Z. Palová),
xxxx.sk (A. Haas),
Michel Wirth (J. Zoričák),
archive SNG,
archive 1. Slovak Invest Company, Bratislava,
Jonker – Zaremba collection, The Netherlands,
Archive autors.
Graphic Design: Bibira Milota Marková
Print: Colorprint Bratislava

Acknowledgments:
Authors for providing Gallery NOVA the rights to publish the photographs.
Slovak National Gallery, Bratislava;
1. Slovak Invest Company, Bratislava;
Jonker – Zaremba collection, The Netherlands;
Dan Klein, Agáta Žačková, Sabina Jankovičová and Vladimíra Büngerová.

Gallery NOVA
Baštová 2, 811 03 Bratislava
www.galeria-nova.sk

isbn 978-80-969285-4-5
ean 9788096928545